Global Insurance Market Trends 2024

OECD

BETTER POLICIES FOR BETTER LIVES

Please cite this publication as:
OECD (2024), *Global Insurance Market Trends 2024*, OECD Publishing, Paris, https://doi.org/10.1787/5b740371-en.

ISBN 978-92-64-92299-0 (print)
ISBN 978-92-64-71882-1 (PDF)
ISBN 978-92-64-81555-1 (HTML)

Global Insurance Market Trends
ISSN 3006-8320 (print)
ISSN 3006-8339 (online)

Photo credits: Cover © Eightshot Studio/Getty Images.

Corrigenda to OECD publications may be found at: https://www.oecd.org/en/publications/support/corrigenda.html.

Foreword

This 2024 edition of the OECD's Global Insurance Market Trends provides an overview and assessment of developments in the insurance industry in 2023, using data from the OECD Global Insurance Statistics (GIS) database.

For several decades, the OECD has collected and analysed data on insurance markets in member countries, including on the number of active companies and their employees, insurance premiums and payments, and portfolio investments. Over time, the framework for this global statistical exercise has come to include key items from the balance sheet and income statement of direct insurers and reinsurers.

The geographical reach of the GIS database has expanded over time. In addition to OECD countries, it also covers a number of non-OECD Latin American (through co-operation with the Association of Latin American Insurance Supervisors, ASSAL), Asian and other jurisdictions.

The *Global Insurance Market Trends* report and GIS database provide a rich source of comparable cross-country data on insurance markets. They provide a comprehensive source of information that can be used by governmental authorities, the insurance sector, the research community, and consumers.

This report has been developed by the Capital Markets and Financial Institutions Division of the OECD Directorate for Financial and Enterprise Affairs. It was prepared by Romain Despalins and Timothy Bishop under the supervision of Pablo Antolin, Head of the Insurance and Pensions Unit, and Serdar Celik, Head of Division. Leigh Wolfrom and Sally Day-Hanotiaux provided input.

Table of contents

Foreword 3

Executive summary 6

1 The insurance business is unevenly developed around the world, with lower coverage in less advanced economies 8

1.1. The penetration of the insurance industry varies widely around the world 9
1.2. The non-life sector generally dominates the insurance industry, with the largest share of premiums 10
1.3. Life insurance business is more prominent in regions with higher per capita income 12

2 Premium growth in the non-life sector led to positive underwriting performance in many cases, despite continued cost pressures 15

2.1. Non-life premiums grew in all reporting jurisdictions 16
2.2. Non-life insurers continued to face higher claims costs 19
2.3. Despite the rise in gross claims payments, non-life insurers generally recorded positive underwriting results 21
2.4. Reinsurance prices increased 23

3 Premium growth in the life sector remained stable overall, but some jurisdictions still witnessed negative trends 25

3.1. While premium growth remained stable and positive overall in the life sector, it nonetheless declined in a number of jurisdictions 26
3.2. Payouts from the life insurance sector continued due to a higher interest rate environment, among other factors 27

4 The investment performance of insurers turned positive due to developments in financial markets 29

4.1. Bonds accounted for over half of the assets of insurers at end-2023 30
4.2. Positive trends in financial markets allowed insurers to improve their investment performance 31

5 The profitability of insurers broadly improved, with previous negative performance generally reversed 33

5.1. The profitability of insurers broadly improved in 2023 34
5.2. Insurer shareholder equity generally increased 34

References 37

Annex A. Statistical tables 39

Annex B. Methodological notes 44

Notes 45

FIGURES

Figure 1.1. Total direct gross premiums written in 2023 9
Figure 1.2. Non-life insurance penetration and GDP per capita in selected jurisdictions in 2023 10
Figure 1.3. Direct gross premiums written by main non-life insurance classes in 2023 11
Figure 1.4. Life insurance penetration and GDP per capita in selected jurisdictions in 2023 12
Figure 2.1. Annual growth rates of direct gross premiums written in the non-life sector in 2023 16
Figure 2.2. Nominal growth rate of direct gross premiums written in selected main non-life insurance classes in 2023 17
Figure 2.3. Nominal growth rate of the price of insurance policies in selected OECD countries in 2023 18
Figure 2.4. Annual growth rates of gross claims payments in the non-life sector in 2023 20
Figure 2.5. Combined ratio for the non-life sector in 2022 and 2023 22
Figure 2.6. Retention ratios in the non-life sector in 2022-23 24
Figure 3.1. Annual growth rates of direct gross premiums written in the life sector in 2023 26
Figure 4.1. Average asset allocation of domestic life, non-life and composite insurers among reporting jurisdictions, at end-2023 30
Figure 4.2. Average real net investment rates of return by type of domestic insurer in selected jurisdictions in 2023 31
Figure 5.1. Return on equity by type of insurer in 2023 34
Figure 5.2. Change in shareholder equity by type of insurer in 2023 35

TABLES

Table A A.1. Asset allocation of domestic life insurers in main instruments or vehicles, at end-2023 39
Table A A.2. Asset allocation of domestic non-life insurers in main instruments or vehicles, at end-2023 40
Table A A.3. Asset allocation of domestic composite insurers in main instruments or vehicles, at end-2023 41
Table A A.4. Average nominal and real net investment rates of return by type of domestic insurer in 2022 and 2023 42

Executive summary

Insurers have been operating in an environment of higher inflation and interest rates in recent years, although inflation started to fall in 2023 and investors were expecting cuts in interest rates. Against this backdrop, the 2024 edition of the *Global Insurance Market Trends* series explores the overall performance and health of the insurance industry in 2023. It first assesses the importance of the insurance sector within the economy across reporting jurisdictions. It then examines premiums and claims trends in the non-life sector in 2023, and non-life underwriting performance, as well as trends in premiums and payouts in the life sector. This edition examines the investment performance and profitability of insurers in 2023.

The insurance business is unevenly developed around the world, with lower coverage in less advanced economies

The penetration of the insurance industry, which is measured as premiums written as a percentage of GDP, varies considerably around the world, with penetration levels generally higher in more advanced and wealthier economies. While premiums written exceeded 10% of GDP in France, the United Kingdom, the United States and some other European and Asian jurisdictions, premiums accounted for a much lower proportion of GDP in many Latin American countries and some European countries. Non-life insurance business is generally the dominant sector within jurisdictions, accounting for the largest portion of premiums written on average around the world, due especially to motor vehicle insurance that is generally mandatory. Life insurance tends to be more developed in jurisdictions with a higher per capita income, where customers may have higher demand for life insurance products.

The prices of non-life insurance policies rose in response to continued cost pressures

Insurers faced increased costs pressures, reflecting inflation in claims costs and the hardening of reinsurance markets. Cost pressures led to increases in premium rates in the main non-life classes (motor vehicle, health and property insurance), which contributed to the growth of premiums written in the non-life sector. Premiums written grew by 12.4% on average in nominal terms in 2023 and 6.2% in real terms, double the real growth rate in 2022. In most jurisdictions, the non-life sector registered positive underwriting performance.

Higher interest rates have had mixed effects on the life insurance sector

The increase in interest rates had direct and indirect impacts on the life insurance sector, with positive and negative effects. In the context of higher interest rates, individuals could expect a higher income from annuity products and higher rates from guaranteed life investment products, which in a number of jurisdictions led to an increased demand for these products, and a shift away from non-guaranteed products where policyholders bear the investment risk. In some jurisdictions, higher interest rates led some customers to surrender their life insurance policies and redeploy their savings, for instance into other financial products or to support the purchase of a home. Higher interest rates also translated into higher mortgage rates, increasing the cost of credit in housing markets and reducing the number of transactions and loans. This has had an indirect impact on the sale of life protection products in those jurisdictions where credit institutions require borrowers to purchase such products. Gross written premiums in the life sector grew overall in nominal terms, in just over two thirds of reporting jurisdictions.

The investment performance of insurers turned positive following developments in financial markets

Insurers achieved a positive investment rate of return in real terms in around two thirds of the reporting jurisdictions. This contrasts with 2022 when in nearly all jurisdictions insurers had negative real investment rates of return due to rising interest rates and falling equity valuations. Falling government bond yields toward the end of 2023, reflecting reduced inflationary expectations, positively impacted bond valuations. Global equity markets also demonstrated strong performance in 2023. These financial market developments boosted the overall investment performance of insurers.

The profitability of insurers broadly improved, with any previous negative performance generally reversed

Insurer industry profitability in 2023 broadly improved, reflecting positive underwriting performance and investment gains. The negative profitability experienced in one or more sectors (life, non-life and/or composite) in some jurisdictions in 2022 was for the most part reversed. These gains contributed to the increase in the shareholder equity of insurers. Many jurisdictions, especially in Europe, started implementing new accounting standards in 2023 (IFRS 17), which has had implications for the recorded liabilities of insurers and their shareholder equity.

1 The insurance business is unevenly developed around the world, with lower coverage in less advanced economies

This section provides a snapshot of the insurance business globally. It first shows the penetration of the insurance sector within the economy across jurisdictions. It then provides a breakdown of the main classes of non-life insurance, which in many jurisdictions is the main branch of the insurance business. This section finally examines where life insurance business is more prominent and what types of life products are available.

1.1. The penetration of the insurance industry varies widely around the world

The importance of the insurance industry within the economy varies considerably across jurisdictions. Insurance penetration, which is the ratio of premiums written over GDP, is a traditional indicator of the development of the insurance business (Kwon and Wolfrom, 2017[1]). Insurance penetration was the highest in some of the largest economies (e.g. France, the United Kingdom, the United States) and some other jurisdictions, mainly in Europe and Asia in 2023 (Figure 1.1). By contrast, insurance penetration was generally lower among Latin American countries (MAPFRE, 2022[2]). Low insurance penetration could reflect a potential lack of financial protection of people and businesses against certain risks for which insurers can provide coverage.

Figure 1.1. Total direct gross premiums written in 2023

As a percentage of GDP

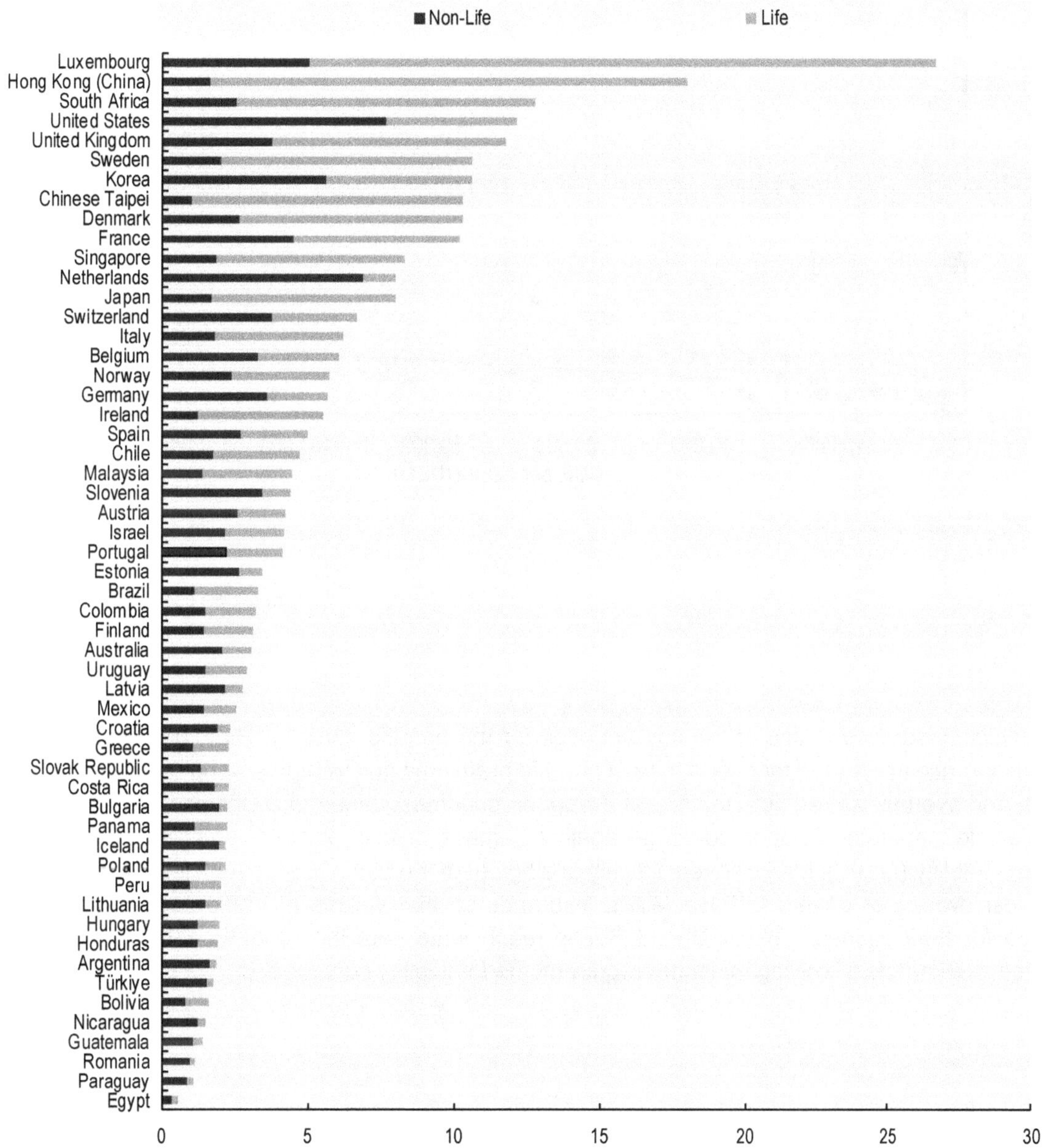

Source: OECD Global Insurance Statistics.

StatLink https://stat.link/en0o1i

1.2. The non-life sector generally dominates the insurance industry, with the largest share of premiums

The non-life sector is generally the largest segment of the insurance industry, accounting on average for the largest share of premiums written. Non-life insurance covers many risks that corporations and individuals may face (e.g. vehicles, property, belongings). Premiums written for non-life insurance accounted for 55% of total premiums written in 2023 on average among the 54 reporting jurisdictions. Some jurisdictions recorded a much higher share of premiums written for non-life insurance, exceeding 80% of total premiums (e.g. Bulgaria, Croatia, Romania). The economic performance of jurisdictions, measured by GDP per capita, has a positive but small impact on the penetration of non-life insurance, which generally remains below 5% of GDP (Figure 1.2).

Figure 1.2. Non-life insurance penetration and GDP per capita in selected jurisdictions in 2023

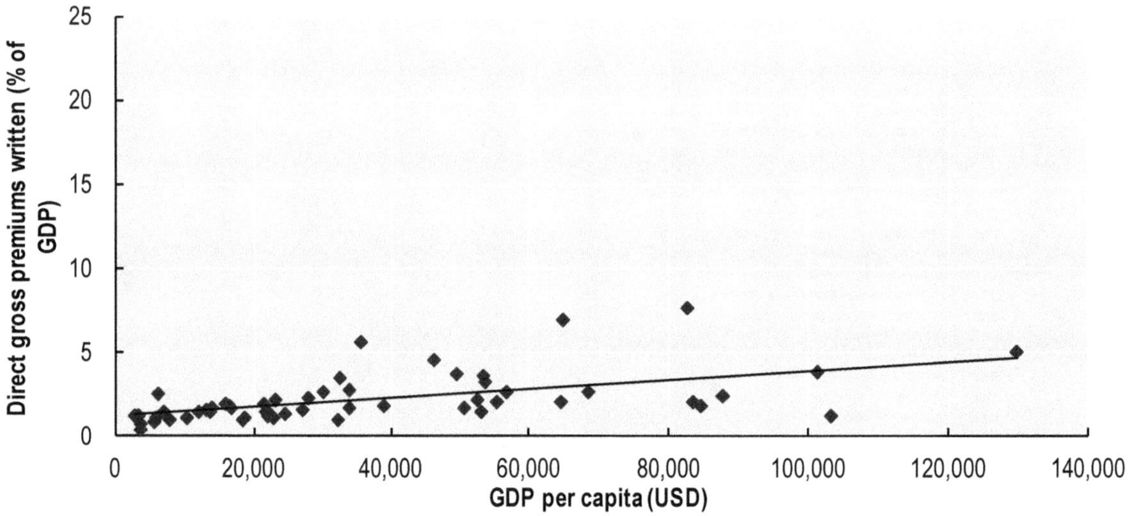

Source: OECD Global Insurance Statistics and IMF.

StatLink https://stat.link/c0d8b3

Motor vehicle insurance is one of the key activities for the non-life industry. Premiums written for motor vehicle insurance accounted for over a third of non-life premiums on average among reporting jurisdictions in 2023, and even exceeded 50% in several European countries, Japan and Chinese Taipei (Figure 1.3). Motor vehicle insurance includes coverage against damage or loss of motor vehicles as well as motor third-party liability (MTPL). MTPL covers liability arising out of the use of motor vehicles. Many jurisdictions require car owners or drivers to have MTPL insurance so that victims of traffic accidents can receive coverage for their injuries.[1] In the United States, each state sets the requirements for motor vehicle insurance, with nearly all having minimum requirements for liability coverage.[2]

Figure 1.3. Direct gross premiums written by main non-life insurance classes in 2023

As a percentage of total gross premiums

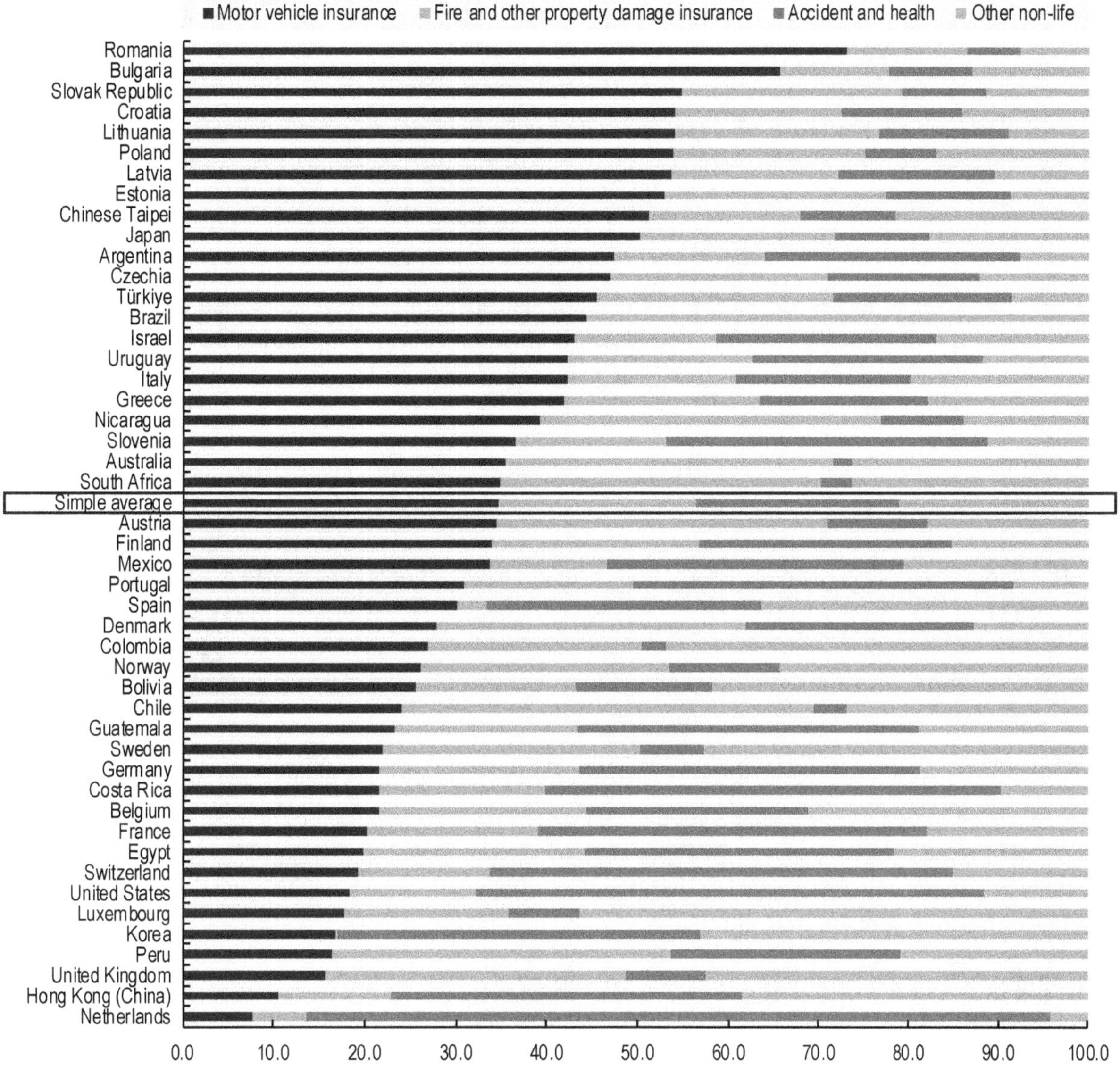

Note: For Korea, "Fire and other property damage insurance" only covers fire insurance; other property damage insurance is under "Other non-life". "Accident and health insurance" for Korea reflects both protection and the savings component of Korean accident and health insurance products.
Source: OECD Global Insurance Statistics.

StatLink https://stat.link/i493an

Health insurance is also a major class of non-life insurance. Premiums written for accident and health insurance accounted for 23% of non-life premiums on average in 2023 among reporting jurisdictions. In a few countries, such as the Netherlands and Switzerland (OECD, 2022[3]), private health insurance is the primary mechanism through which health care coverage is obtained. In most countries, private health insurance plays a secondary role.[3] Private health insurance is generally voluntary with some exceptions (e.g. Chile, France, Germany, Netherlands, Switzerland).[4] Private health insurance coverage is high in countries mandating participation in private health insurance (for instance in France, the Netherlands and

Switzerland where nearly all the population is covered (OECD, 2023[4])) and countries with no public universal healthcare such as in the United States.[5] This high proportion of people with private health insurance coverage helps to explain to some extent the large share of accident and health insurance within total non-life premiums written in these jurisdictions (82% in the Netherlands, 56% in the United States, 51% in Switzerland, 43% in France).

Fire and other property damage insurance is also a significant segment in the non-life sector. Fire insurance is a type of property insurance covering damages and losses caused by fire. Property insurance provides coverage against fire, theft and other threats to assets and equipment in private houses and companies. Property insurance can include different types of policies (e.g. homeowners insurance, renters insurance). Customers of property insurance include landlords, homeowners, and tenants.[6] Property insurance may be a condition to obtain a loan when homeowners take out a mortgage.[7]

Other non-life lines of insurance include other personal and commercial insurance policies, such as transport/freight insurance and travel insurance. Premiums written for these other policies can be significant. For example, in Luxembourg, marine, aviation and other transport insurance accounted for over 20% of premiums written in the non-life sector in 2023, highlighting its role in specialty insurance.

1.3. Life insurance business is more prominent in regions with higher per capita income

The life insurance sector is generally more prominent in advanced economies. Life insurance traditionally offers protection against risks affecting the policyholder directly but it can also provide a contractual vehicle for investment and savings. Life insurance includes various types of products (see Box 1.1 at the end of this section). Individuals may purchase life insurance on their own (individual insurance) or get coverage through their employer (group insurance).

In 2023, the share of life premiums written exceeded 75% of total premiums written in advanced economies in Asia (Hong Kong (China), Japan, Chinese Taipei, Singapore) and several European countries (Ireland, Luxembourg, Sweden). Advanced economies generally have a high level of income per capita. Life insurance penetration increases with GDP per capita (more strongly than for non-life insurance), although with some variability at higher levels of GDP per capita (Figure 1.4). In wealthier jurisdictions, individuals have higher incomes and are thus more able to afford life insurance products.

Figure 1.4. Life insurance penetration and GDP per capita in selected jurisdictions in 2023

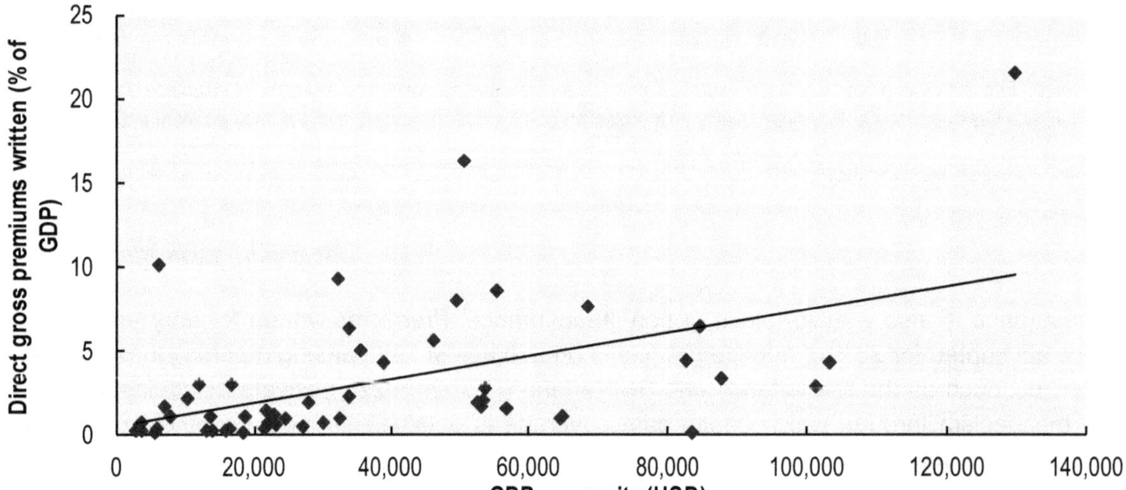

Source: OECD Global Insurance Statistics and IMF.

StatLink https://stat.link/3bzk6n

Individual life insurance policies that pay benefits upon the death of the policyholder are the most popular life insurance products among some advanced economies in Asia. For example, most of the life insurance premiums were for whole life insurance in Hong Kong (China), individual insurance policies in Japan (in particular term insurance and whole life) and endowment policies in Chinese Taipei.[8] Premiums written for life insurance products were also significant in the United States (especially whole life insurance with USD 67 billion in net premiums in 2023), although not as large as for annuity products (USD 360 billion). Life insurance products such as whole life and term insurance may be used as a financial tool for protecting the financial well-being of families in the event of the death of the insured person.

Population ageing and the design of the payout of asset-backed pensions can also support the demand for annuity products.[9] Life annuity products provide a regular stream of income to retirees. They can protect retirees against longevity risk, which is the risk that people live longer than expected and as a result outlive their retirement savings. All OECD countries offer the option of receiving retirement benefits as a lifetime income. This option is mandatory for several occupational plans and mandatory for personal pension schemes (e.g. Denmark, Sweden). Adverse selection may reduce or limit the take up of annuities in voluntary markets, as annuities may appear expensive for an individual who may have a lower life expectancy than a typical annuitant (Fong and Li, 2022[5]). While life annuity products are not available in Costa Rica due to a lack of annuity markets, annuities are nevertheless a possible payout option from mandatory personal pension plans (IMF, 2024[6]).

Unit-linked products have become increasingly common in some jurisdictions as insurers have moved away from insurance products with promised rates of return or guarantees providing downside investment protection. For example, in Israel, unit-linked premiums accounted for more than 60% of premiums written in the life sector in 2023. Unit-linked products give policyholders access to investment funds and allow them to select from a range of different funds based on their investment objectives and tolerance for risk. Policyholders often bear the investment risks for this type of product and thus returns can be volatile.

Box 1.1. Life insurance products

Life insurance includes a variety of products, such as:

- *Whole life insurance*: It pays benefits to beneficiaries upon the death of the policyholder. This insurance provides coverage throughout the life of the policyholder.
- *Term insurance*: It provides a guaranteed payment to beneficiaries upon the death of the policyholder if the policyholder dies during the term specified in the contract.
- *Endowment policies*: These policies provide a payment after a specific term (maturity of the contract) or at the death of the policyholder.
- *Annuity contracts*: These products offer a stream of income payments to individuals (e.g. upon retirement). Insurers may offer different types of annuity contracts with different types of payments, such as fixed payments, indexed payments (e.g. on inflation, profits) (OECD, 2016[7]).
- *Unit-linked products*: The policy gives different investment options to policyholders who typically bear the investment risk but also benefit from the potential investment gains in financial markets.

Individuals may obtain coverage in different ways. For instance, they may purchase a life insurance product on their own (individual insurance) or get coverage through their employer (group insurance).

Credit institutions may require individuals seeking to obtain a loan to purchase certain forms of life insurance (e.g. term insurance). These products can help to pay off the outstanding balance on a debt if the borrower dies before fully repaying it.

2 Premium growth in the non-life sector led to positive underwriting performance in many cases, despite continued cost pressures

This section assesses the underwriting performance of the non-life sector in 2023. It looks at the growth of premiums and gross claims payments over the period. It then examines the combined ratio (the excess of claims paid or incurred and operating expenses over premiums) to assess whether insurers achieved underwriting gains. Finally, it discusses reinsurance prices and its effect on the take up of reinsurance by direct insurers.

2.1. Non-life premiums grew in all reporting jurisdictions

Gross premiums written in the non-life sector grew in nominal terms in all reporting jurisdictions in 2023, by 12.4% on average (Figure 2.1), slightly below the nominal growth rate in 2022 (14.1% on average) (OECD, 2023[8]). Gross premiums written generally grew faster than consumer prices in 2023, with a few exceptions (Finland, Japan, Luxembourg), thus leading to growth in real terms. The premium growth rate in real terms doubled, from 2.9% in 2022 to 6.2% in 2023 on average.

Figure 2.1. Annual growth rates of direct gross premiums written in the non-life sector in 2023

In per cent

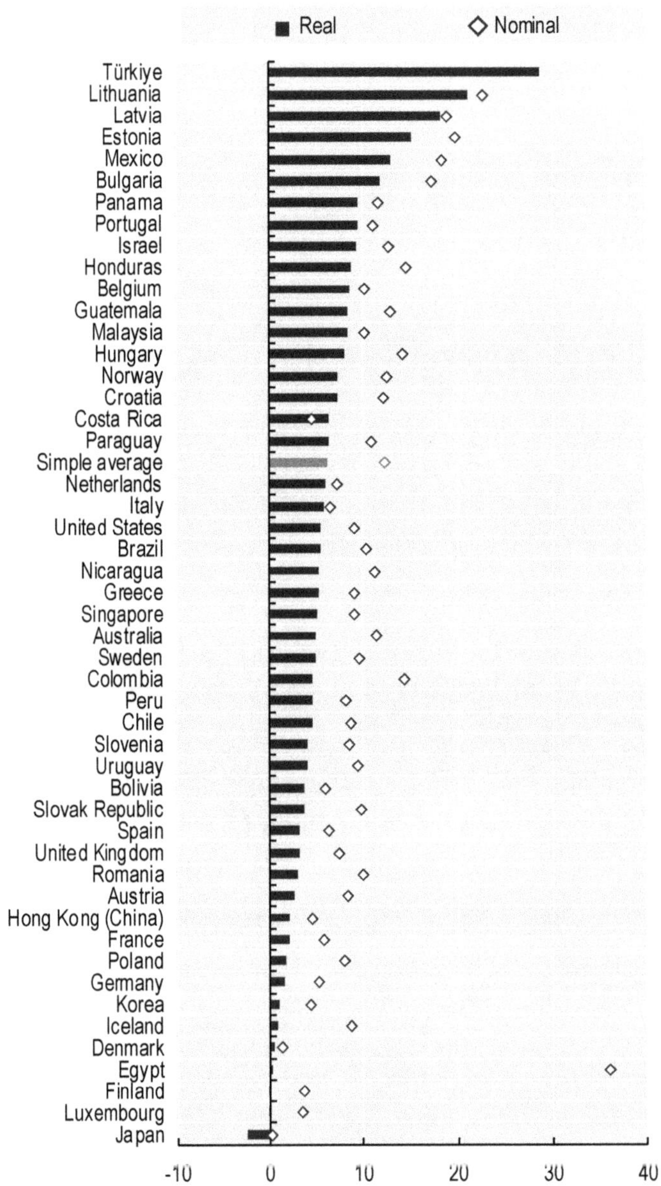

Note: Data refer to the gross premiums written in the non-life sector for all undertakings (i.e. domestic undertakings and branches and agencies of foreign undertakings operating in the reporting jurisdiction) except when only data on domestic undertakings are available. The nominal premium growth rate is not shown for Türkiye (112.1%) for readability purposes.
Source: OECD Global Insurance Statistics.

StatLink https://stat.link/me9lht

The nominal growth of non-life premiums was visible across the main non-life insurance classes. In nearly all reporting jurisdictions, gross premiums grew in nominal terms for motor vehicle, fire and other property damage and accident and health (Figure 2.2).

Figure 2.2. Nominal growth rate of direct gross premiums written in selected main non-life insurance classes in 2023

In per cent

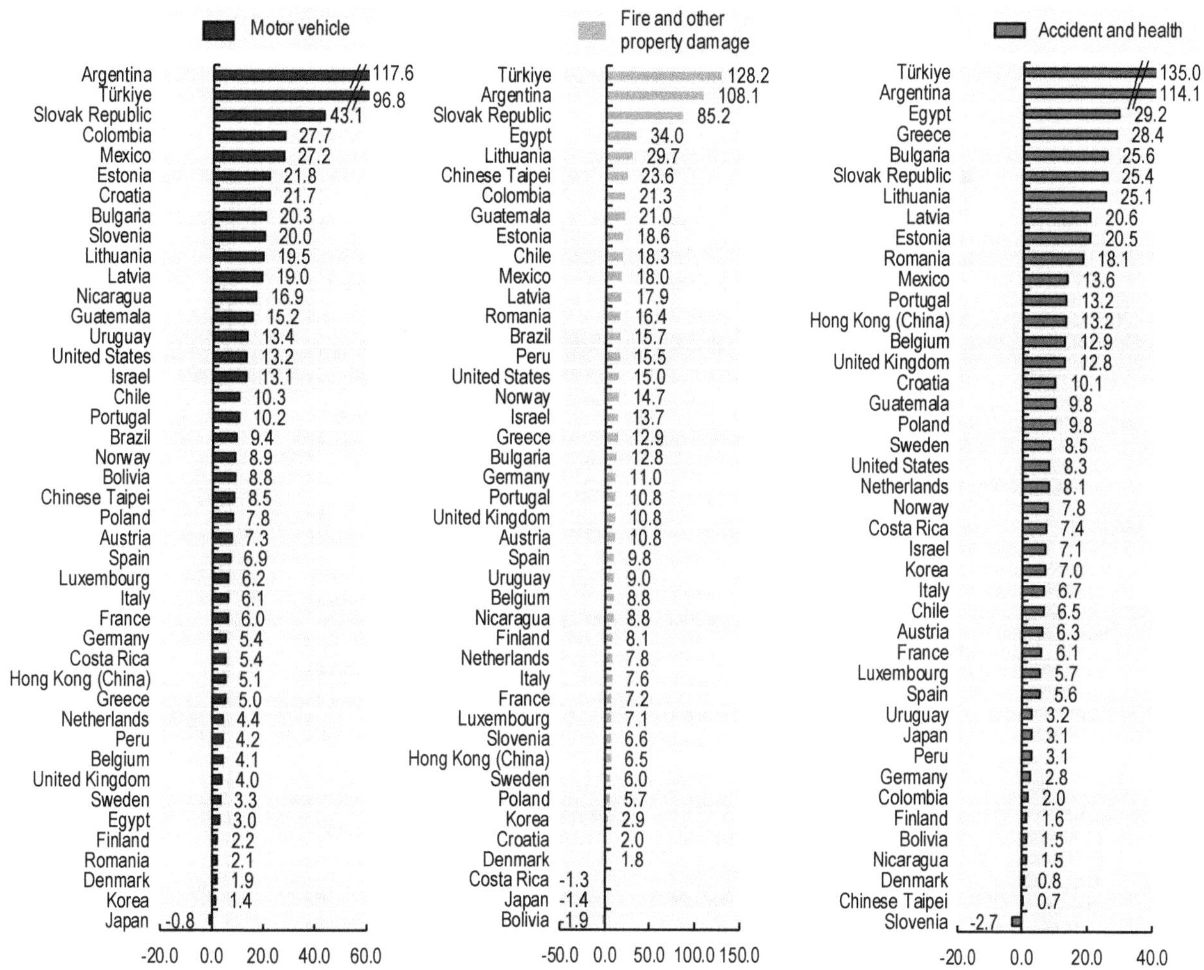

Note: For Korea, "Fire and other property damage insurance" only covers fire insurance. "Accident and health insurance" for Korea reflects both protection and the savings component of Korean accident and health insurance products.
Source: OECD Global Insurance Statistics.

StatLink https://stat.link/6ealr3

The growth of non-life premiums was partly attributable to an increase in the number of non-life insurance policies. Car sales increased in some jurisdictions (e.g. Croatia, Mexico, Malaysia), supporting the demand for motor vehicle insurance.[10] More generally, the economic recovery following the COVID-19 pandemic has boosted the demand for insurance coverage. Some supervisors also attributed the growth in the number of insurance policies to an increased awareness of the population about the need for insurance protection (e.g. property insurance in Lithuania due to recent disaster events). Finland also recorded an increased demand for voluntary health insurance due to new products enabled by technology and because of concerns over the availability of public health care services.

The increase in gross premiums written in nominal terms across the main non-life insurance classes was also the result of increasing prices of non-life insurance policies. Insurance policy prices increased in 2023 in most OECD countries and across all the main classes of insurance, and in some cases significantly (Figure 2.3).

Figure 2.3. Nominal growth rate of the price of insurance policies in selected OECD countries in 2023

In per cent

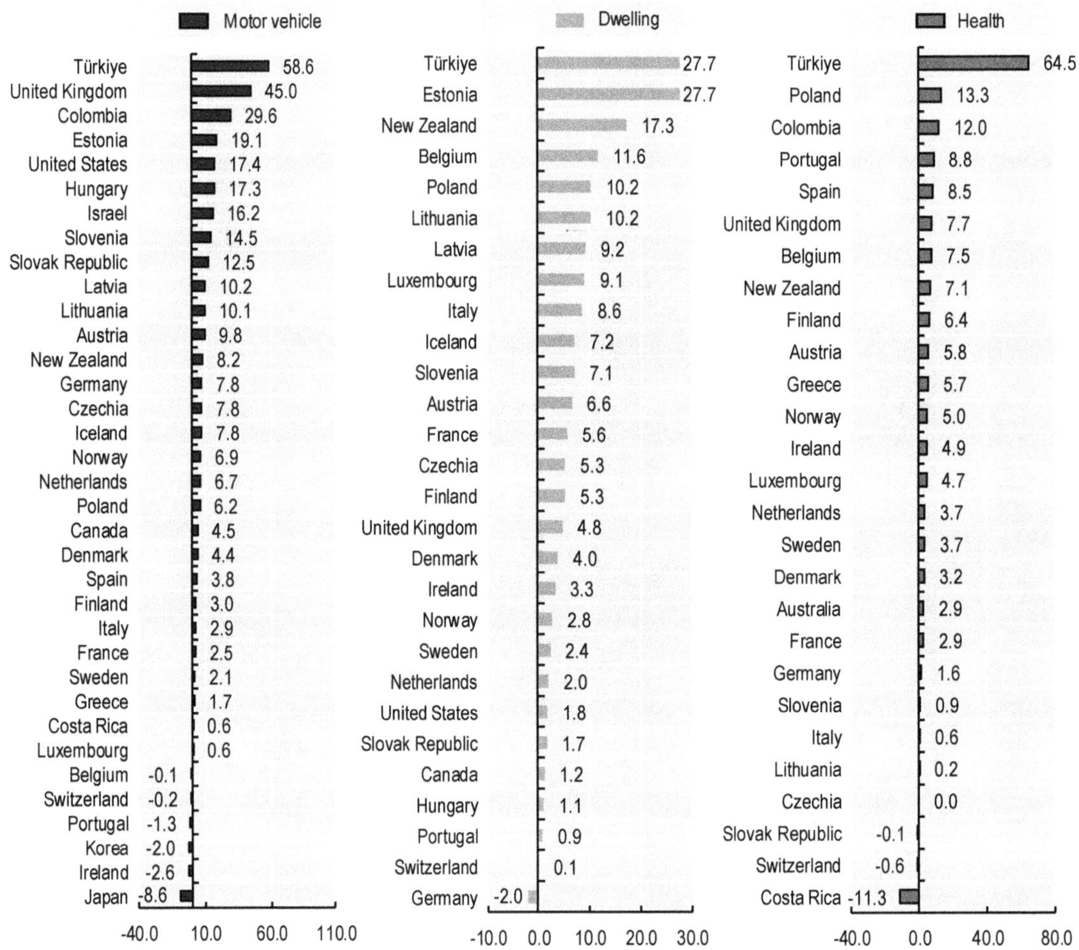

Note: Data for dwelling insurance for Canada refer to tenants' insurance premiums; data for motor vehicle insurance refer to passenger vehicle insurance premiums. Data for health insurance in Norway and Türkiye are for insurance connected with health; data for motor vehicle insurance are for insurance connected with transport. For Portugal, data in the first panel refer only to insurance connected with transport (including vehicle insurance, freight insurance) instead of motor vehicle insurance. Data for the United States show a U.S. city average for all urban consumers.
Source: Australia's Department of Health and Aged Care; Eurostat; Statistics Canada; DANE (Colombia); INEC (Costa Rica); Israel's Central Bureau of Statistics; Statistics of Japan; Korean Statistical Information Service; Statistics New Zealand; ONS (United Kingdom); United States Bureau of Labor Statistics.

StatLink https://stat.link/h3pxb8

The increase in prices in 2023 is due to larger claims payments that insurers in most jurisdictions faced in 2022 (OECD, 2023[8]). Insurers have passed on some of these costs to customers through higher policy rates. In only a few cases has the price of insurance policies remained stable or even declined, due for instance to a lower frequency of claim events than in the past (e.g. motor vehicle insurance in Japan),[11] competitive pressures (e.g. motor vehicle insurance in Korea)[12] or regulatory caps (e.g. health insurance in Slovenia).[13] Competitive pressures and regulation may prevent insurers from raising the prices of insurance policies to adjust for rising claims costs.

The increase in prices of insurance policies could increase the risk of widening insurance protection gaps. The price of some non-life insurance policies increased more than the overall amount of gross premiums written in some countries. For example, in the United Kingdom, the price of motor vehicle insurance grew by 45% in 2023 while gross premiums written for motor vehicle insurance only grew by 4% in nominal terms. Increased insurance pricing and the rising cost of living may have led policyholders to reduce the amount or the scope of cover (for example moving from comprehensive policies with extras, to core cover, or with higher levels of excess or deductibles).

2.2. Non-life insurers continued to face higher claims costs

Non-life insurers continued to face higher claims costs in 2023. While gross claims payments increased by 17% in nominal terms in 2022 (OECD, 2023[8]), they grew again by around 17% on average among 49 jurisdictions in 2023 (Figure 2.4). This is more than the growth rate of consumer price indices in 2023 – in real terms, the growth in claims payments almost doubled on average, from 5.5% to 10.1%.

Figure 2.4. Annual growth rates of gross claims payments in the non-life sector in 2023

In per cent

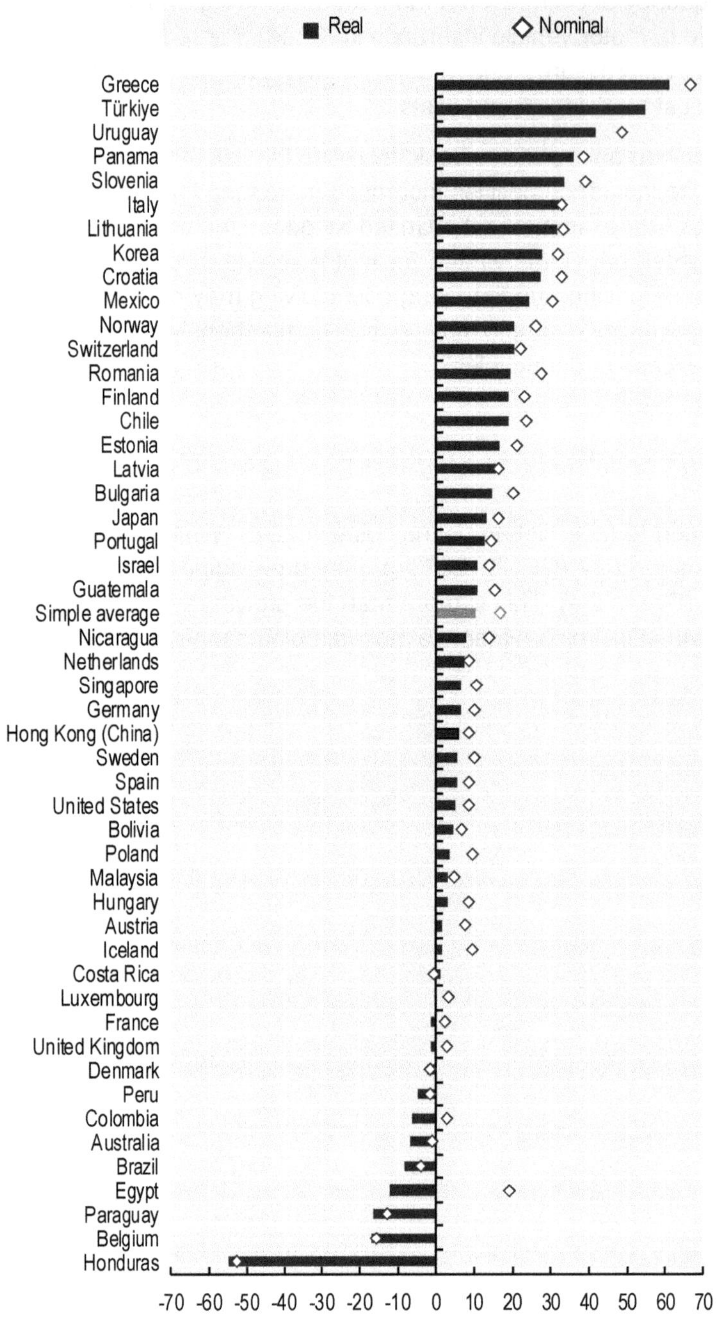

Note: Growth rates of gross claims payments take into account the variations in outstanding claims provisions (when this information is available) to reflect better the magnitude of the obligations that the industry had in 2023 as a result of insured events that occurred. When the breakdown of gross claims paid or changes in claims outstanding provisions for composite undertakings into their life and non-life businesses was not available, the breakdown in each subsector was assumed to be the same as for gross premiums written. The nominal growth rate of claims paid is not shown for Türkiye (155.3%) for readability purposes.
Source: OECD Global Insurance Statistics.

StatLink https://stat.link/9357ki

The continued increase in claims costs was a combination of several factors, including rising prices and a higher frequency or higher cost of claim events. Prices continued to increase in 2023, although they increased at a slower pace than in 2022 (IMF, 2024[9]). The rise in prices affects multiple lines of business (e.g. motor vehicle, health, property). The costs of car repairs increased due to higher costs of material and labour (e.g. United States).[14] Medical expenses (e.g. drugs, hospitalisation) also increased, accounting to some extent for the growth in gross claims payments in France and Slovenia. The increase in claims payments was also due to a higher frequency of claim events in a number of countries such as Denmark, Finland, Lithuania, Nicaragua and Norway. The surge in car sales in Nicaragua and the higher incidence of traffic accidents led to a surge in claims payments. Norway also recorded a higher frequency of claims for motor insurance, assistance and property, which drove up claims payments. Countries that recorded an increase in the number of policies are also likely to record a larger number of claim events.

Natural hazards led to higher claims payments in 2023 in different countries and regions. For example, non-life claims payments surged in 2023 following floods in central Greece, a hurricane in Mexico, a landslide and storm in Norway, storms and floods in Slovenia, an earthquake in Türkiye, and a drought in Uruguay. Swiss Re (2024[10]) estimates that the number of insured natural catastrophes reached a new record in 2023, although these catastrophes generated lower economic losses overall in 2023 than in 2022. The increased frequency of severe storms also contributed to the rise in claims costs for property and casualty in the United States (NAIC, 2024[11]). Insurers in Portugal continued to pay claims in 2023 for the multiple floods in Lisbon in December 2022.

Insurers in some jurisdictions experienced a return to lower claim payments after settling payments for major high-cost events, such as natural hazards and the COVID-19 pandemic. Insurers experienced a reduction in claims payments from natural hazards in 2023 after large payments in Australia (for individual and commercial property insurance from the 2022 flooding event in New South Wales and Southeast Queensland) and Honduras (final payments in 2022 for claims related to storm Eta and Iota in 2020). Japan also recorded a lower occurrence of severe natural hazards in 2023. In Chinese Taipei, the claims of the non-life insurance industry in 2023 were down by 36.4% compared to 2022, primarily due to a decrease in claims payments related to COVID-19.

Legislative changes can also affect trends in claims payments. For example, a legislative amendment in Finland removed several examinations and treatments by private doctors from the scope of reimbursements from the public health care system (Daily Finland, 2022[12]). This development, combined with the increased demand for private health insurance (Yle, 2024[13]) may have accounted for the increase in payments from insurers in 2023. In Lithuania, amendment of the Law on compulsory insurance against civil liability related to the use of motor vehicles at end-2023 broadened the definition of vehicle and increased the minimum obligatory amounts of insurance coverage. This will likely affect payments in this line of business.

2.3. Despite the rise in gross claims payments, non-life insurers generally recorded positive underwriting results

Despite the rise in gross claims payments, non-life insurers recorded underwriting gains in most reporting jurisdictions in 2023. Figure 2.5 shows that the combined ratio was below 100% in most jurisdictions. The combined ratio measures the underwriting profitability of insurance companies in their direct non-life business. It is the aggregate of the loss ratio (which measures claims paid and changes in claims provisions relative to gross premiums) and expense ratio (which measures expenses incurred and commissions relative to gross premiums). A combined ratio of less than 100% represents underwriting gains (also called technical profits) for the insurance industry, which was the case in most jurisdictions, despite the rise in gross claims payments. Insurers experienced an underwriting loss in a few jurisdictions (6 out of the 34 reporting jurisdictions), the largest losses occurring in Chinese Taipei (where claims payments remained high because of COVID-19) and Türkiye (most likely because of the earthquake in early 2023 (Insurance Journal, 2024[14])).

Figure 2.5. Combined ratio for the non-life sector in 2022 and 2023

In per cent

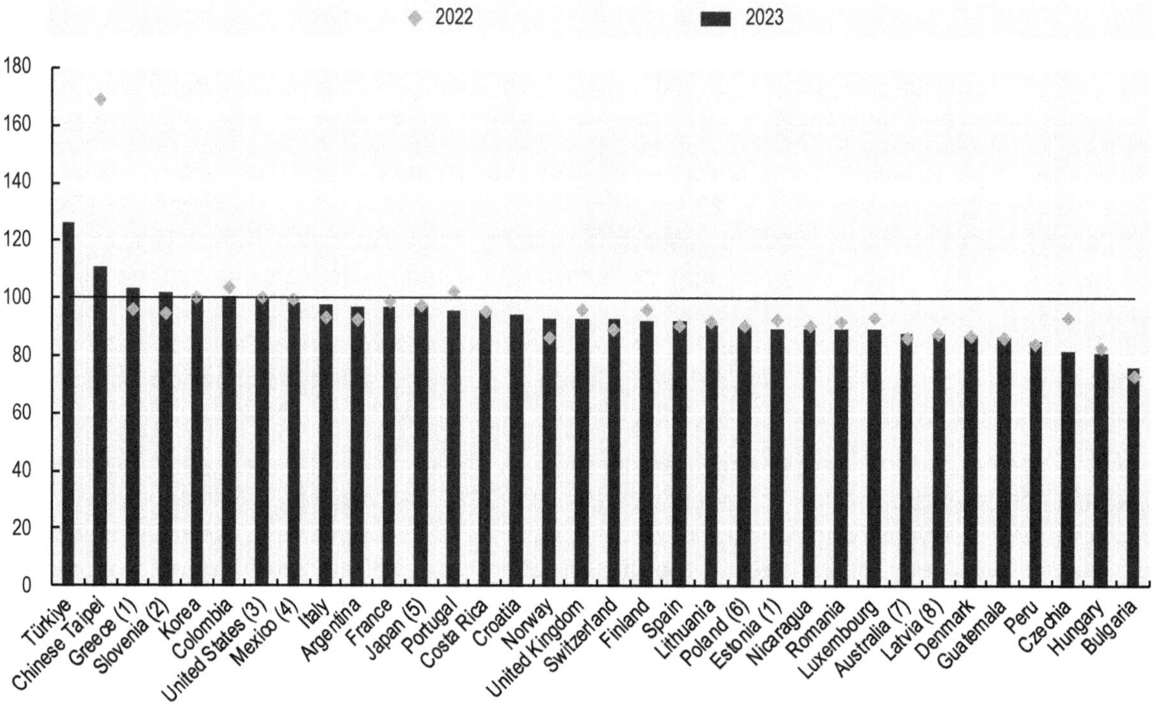

Notes: The combined ratios are the results of the calculations by the respective authorities in the reporting jurisdictions. The underlying formula may therefore be different across jurisdictions.

1. The results are net combined ratios.
2. The result is the sum of the net claims incurred and net operating expenses over net premiums earned.
3. The result is the simple average of the combined ratio of P&C insurance (102.5% in 2022, 101.5% in 2023) and health insurance (97.5% in 2022, 98.2% in 2023).
4. The result is the simple average of the combined ratio of accident and health (96.9% in 2022, 97.7% in 2023) and auto insurance (101.5% in 2022, 99% in 2023).
5. The results are for fiscal years instead of calendar years.
6. The result is the sum of gross claims ratio, acquisition costs ratio and administrative expenses ratio.
7. The results are net underwriting combined ratios for the general insurance industry for years ending in June.
8. Data cover life insurance.

Sources: APRA (Australia); Danish Financial Supervisory Authority (Denmark); ACPR (France): MNB (Hungary); IVASS (Italy); CNSF (Mexico); KNF (Poland); ASF (Portugal); ISA (Slovenia); FINMA (Switzerland); Bank of England (United Kingdom); NAIC (United States); answers to the qualitative questionnaire of the OECD Global Insurance Statistics exercise (all other jurisdictions).

StatLink https://stat.link/im3b8w

Underwriting results varied across lines of business. For example, in Costa Rica, the combined ratio for the non-life sector was below 100% but it exceeded 100% for fire, health, occupational risk and motor vehicle insurance. The median combined ratio for non-life insurers in Europe ranged from below 50% for credit and suretyship insurance to close to 100% for motor vehicle insurance in Q4 2023 (EIOPA, 2024[15]).

In the United Kingdom, the non-life sector had a combined ratio below 100% but many UK motor insurers still had a combined ratio of more than 100% (average of 114%). In the United States, the combined ratio for the non-life sector was below 100% although insurers in homeowner lines recorded underwriting losses due to an above-average frequency of catastrophes (NAIC, 2024[11]).

Despite positive underwriting results for the non-life sector in 2023 across jurisdictions, underwriting profitability fell in 2023 relative to 2022 in close to half of the reporting jurisdictions (14 out of 32). The combined ratio deteriorated the most in Greece, Norway, and Slovenia (by more than 7 percentage points), due to natural hazards (in the three countries) or for other reasons (such as the growth in claims payments for health insurance in Slovenia). These events led to a large growth in gross claims payments, larger than for premium growth.

Where the underwriting profitability of non-life insurers improved relative to 2022, the reasons for the improvement differed across jurisdictions. In some cases, the improvement was driven by claims payments declining (e.g. Costa Rica, Chinese Taipei). In some others, claims payments increased at a lower pace than premiums (e.g. France, United Kingdom, United States). In others, although claims paid increased faster than premiums, the combined ratio improved thanks to a reduction of the expense ratio (e.g. Mexico, Romania).[15] In the case of Finland, the improvement reflected a change in methodology.[16]

Reinsurance can have an effect on underwriting profitability and sectoral trends. For example, in Australia, the combined ratio deteriorated on a net basis despite the decline in gross claims incurred because of a fall in reinsurance recoveries. Finland noted that the increase in reinsurance prices of large international reinsurance companies has affected the profitability of non-life insurance business. In the case of the United States, homeowner insurers bore the brunt of claims payments arising from natural hazards in 2023 since the events did not reach reinsurance limits. This contributed to underwriting losses of homeowner insurers in the United States.

2.4. Reinsurance prices increased

The reinsurance market hardened in 2023 as reinsurance prices increased. Reinsurance prices increased significantly, in particular for property reinsurance cover where pricing increased by between 20% to 60% (Fitch, 2023[16]). This increase is due to both inflation and more frequent and costlier natural hazards, which have led to larger claims payments by direct insurers.

Increased reinsurance pricing may have contributed to an increase in retention ratios in some jurisdictions. The retention ratio is the proportion of premiums – and therefore risk – that insurers retain rather than transfer to reinsurers. The retention ratio was higher in 2023 than in 2022 in 20 out 45 reporting jurisdictions, although the increase tended to be marginal (Figure 2.6). For example, the retention ratio increased from 76.5% in 2022 to 77% in 2023 in Germany, and from 63.9% to 64.1% in the United Kingdom.

Figure 2.6. Retention ratios in the non-life sector in 2022-23

In per cent

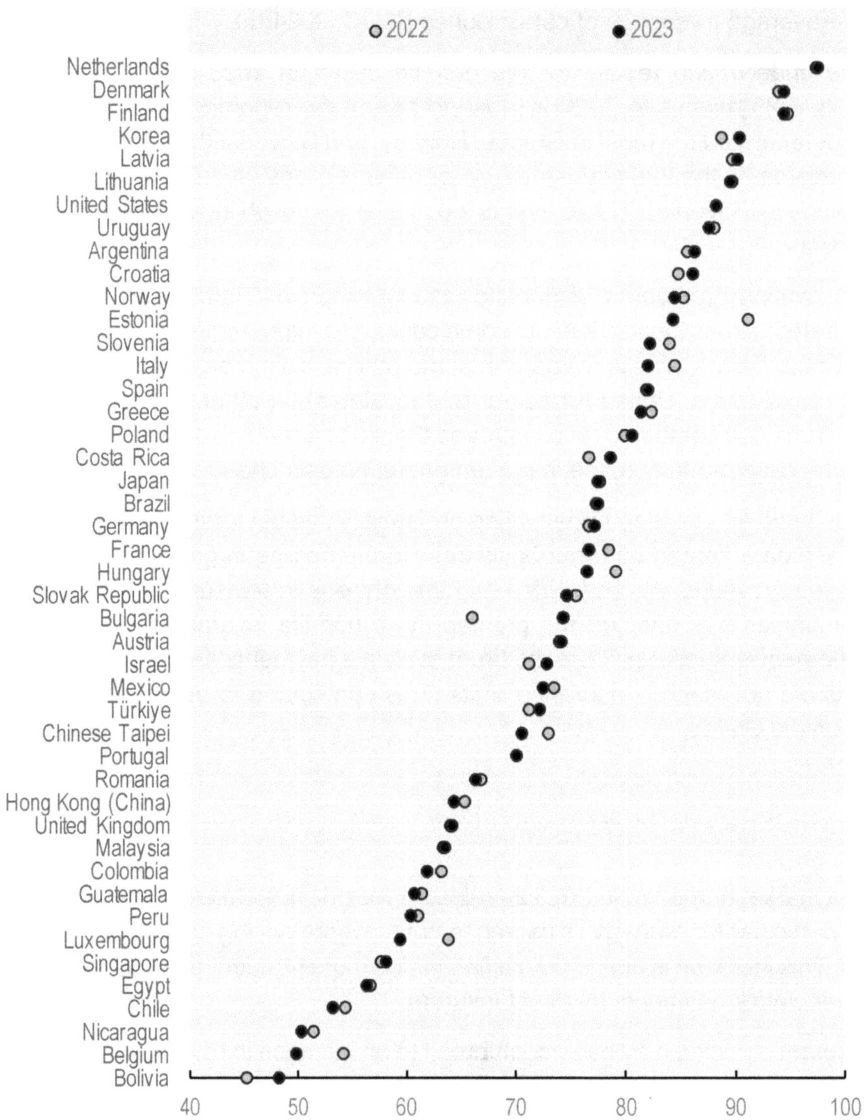

Source: OECD Global Insurance Statistics.

StatLink https://stat.link/w50h68

The hardening of the reinsurance market was also visible in the terms and conditions of reinsurance policies. Czechia noted a restriction of the range of reinsurance coverage offered. Malaysia also noted a hardening of reinsurance terms. Reinsurers may, for example, change the terms by raising the level at which a reinsurance policy pays out (Carrier Management, 2024[17]). Reinsurers may have also been less inclined to reinsure secondary perils (i.e. smaller but more frequent events such as tornadoes, thunderstorms, fire and floods) on which they incurred losses in the recent years (Carrier Management, 2024[17]). In this context, some insurers faced challenges in renewing their reinsurance protection and have had to increase retention levels and take on more risk.

3 Premium growth in the life sector remained stable overall, but some jurisdictions still witnessed negative trends

This section examines the growth rates of premiums and payouts in the life sector. It first shows the growth rates of gross premiums written for life insurance by jurisdiction and then discusses life insurance payouts in 2023.

3.1. While premium growth remained stable and positive overall in the life sector, it nonetheless declined in a number of jurisdictions

In the life sector, gross premiums increased in nominal terms in just over two thirds of the reporting jurisdictions (34 out of 50), with the largest rise occurring in Spain (37%) after Türkiye (83%) (Figure 3.1). By contrast, life business contracted in nominal terms in a number of European countries (e.g. Croatia, Portugal, Luxembourg) and in some Asian jurisdictions (e.g. Korea, Singapore). In real terms (i.e. after adjusting for the changes in consumer prices), business volume was stable on average, with a real growth rate below 1% (versus -3.9% real growth in 2022), although this hides differences in trends across jurisdictions.

Figure 3.1. Annual growth rates of direct gross premiums written in the life sector in 2023

In per cent

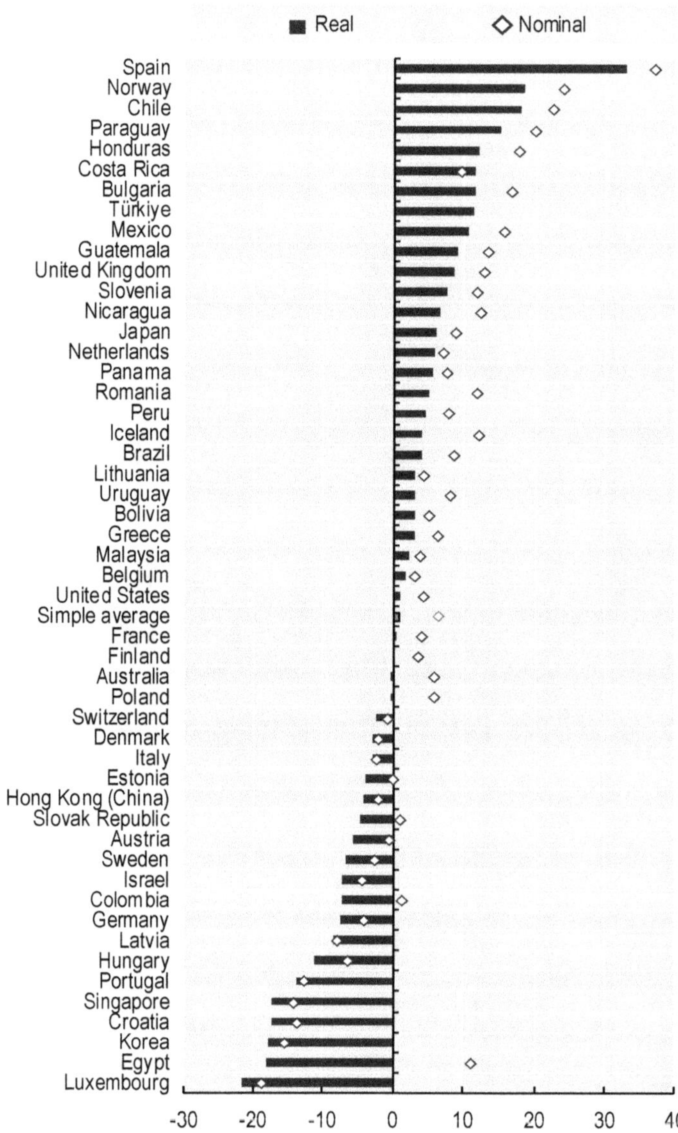

Note: Data refer to the gross premiums written in the life sector for all undertakings (i.e. domestic undertakings and branches and agencies of foreign undertakings operating in the reporting jurisdiction) except when only data on domestic undertakings are available. The nominal premium growth rate is not shown for Türkiye (83.4%) for readability purposes.

Source: OECD Global Insurance Statistics.

StatLink https://stat.link/cgzowt

Trends in gross premiums written varied by type of life insurance product. Annuity products and other guaranteed life investment products generally experienced premium growth. For instance, in the United Kingdom and the United States, the sales of annuity products soared in 2023.[17] In Japan, the fastest growing segment in the life sector was annuities, while in Spain the annuity business grew by 53.7% (Dirección General de Seguros y Fondos de Pensiones, 2024[18]). By contrast, unit-linked products and other products, where policyholders bear the investment risk, experienced more mixed results, with some jurisdictions registering an increased allocation of premiums to these products in 2023 compared to 2022 (e.g. Bulgaria, Estonia, Greece, Lithuania, Romania), while others saw a drop (Hong Kong (China), Poland, Portugal).

The increased interest in annuity products resulted from the higher level of interest rates relative to earlier years. Higher interest rates have made annuity products and other guaranteed life investment products more attractive, both to individuals and corporates. In a context of higher interest rates, individuals could expect higher guarantees from insurers and higher income from these guaranteed products. Some employers have also sought to take advantage of the improving funding position of their pension plans to transfer the liabilities and risks to the insurance sector (OECD, 2024[19]). Insurers have recorded an increase in bulk purchases of annuities from pension schemes (such as in the United Kingdom).

In some jurisdictions, heightened consumer interest in guaranteed products may have occurred at the expense of unit-linked products and other products where policyholders bear some investment risk. For example, in Australia, Hong Kong (China), Poland and Portugal, premiums for non-unit linked products increased while premiums for unit-linked products declined. The elevated volatility in financial markets (e.g. in 2022) may have contributed to the shift away from riskier products, such as in Latvia for unit-linked products and in Chinese Taipei for variable annuities. On the other hand, gross premiums written for unit-linked products increased in some jurisdictions (e.g. Bulgaria).

The decline in premiums for life protection products that some jurisdictions experienced was caused by the downturn in housing markets in 2023. Higher interest rates have translated into higher mortgage lending rates, making it more costly for people to purchase a home, and thus reducing home property transactions and lending. This can have an effect on the demand for life insurance, which banks may request as a condition to provide a mortgage loan. In the United Kingdom, the decline in property sales led to a decline in life protection sales. The decline in premiums for life protection products in Spain could also have been due to a drop in mortgage lending (Dirección General de Seguros y Fondos de Pensiones, 2024[18]).

Several other obstacles weighed on the demand or supply of life insurance products and therefore on the growth of life premiums in general. Australia noted that one of these obstacles was the increase in price of life insurance policies, set against cost-of-living pressures. Another obstacle may be the low perceived value of life insurance products or a lack of consumer confidence, which Slovenia noted as being the case for unit-linked products. On the supply side, Lithuania attributed the decline in the sale of new life insurance contracts to restrictions on commission fees for unit-linked contracts. In Slovenia, insurers have limited the supply of endowment policies. In Switzerland, insurers rarely offer guaranteed products, and when they do, the guarantee is often just a capital guarantee, thus potentially further limiting take-up.

3.2. Payouts from the life insurance sector continued due to a higher interest rate environment, among other factors

The trends in terms of payouts varied widely across jurisdictions and even within regions.[18] Insurers experienced a large increase in payouts in nominal terms in 2023 in some European (e.g. Estonia, Italy,

Luxembourg) and Latin American countries (e.g. Colombia, Nicaragua), and a large decline in some others (e.g. Croatia, Hungary and Poland in the EU, and Bolivia and Paraguay in Latin America).

The rise in interest rates compared to earlier years contributed to an increase in surrenders and thus payouts in life insurance in several countries. Surrenders increased in France, as a result of the rise in interest rates and the rising cost of financing mortgages (ACPR, 2024[20]). According to France's insurance supervisor, policyholders surrendered their policies in order to draw on their savings and purchase a property or help a relative purchase a property. Lithuania also noted an increase in the termination of contracts, which it attributed to elevated inflation and increased consumer demand to draw on savings to finance higher expenses. Luxembourg also recorded a large increase in surrenders, due to the repayment of variable rate loans and a move towards products offering higher yields. In Chinese Taipei, higher interest rates led to an increase in surrenders as policyholders cancelled their life insurance policies in order to purchase other, higher yielding, financial products. Yet some countries reported that surrender rates remained stable (e.g. Netherlands, Slovak Republic); for instance, in the Netherlands, tax penalties for withdrawals from life insurance contracts may have dissuaded people from surrendering their policies despite higher interest rates.

Other factors were behind the increase in payouts. For instance, the evolving conflicts in the Middle East led to a surge in payouts from insurance companies in the region. In Singapore, payments for contracts maturing or anticipated endowments rose in 2023 and accounted for the large share of payments by life insurers.[19] In Estonia, payouts increased due to the end of a 12-year period of tax exemption for unit-linked products, which led to an increase in policyholders opting out of their unit-linked contracts. Increased inflation led to higher payouts for annuity products when benefit payments were partly indexed to inflation. For example, in Colombia, annuity payments are indexed to the consumer price index every year. Additionally, annuity payments (i.e. pensions) in Colombia cannot be lower than the minimum wage and the minimum wage grows more than inflation, which means that the minimum pension that retirees receive increases more than inflation.

Some jurisdictions witnessed lower payouts relative to 2022. For instance, lower mortality in Poland led to fewer payouts and improved technical profits for traditional life insurance. In Croatia, the payouts for unit-linked products declined in line with the shrinking unit-linked business.

4 The investment performance of insurers turned positive due to developments in financial markets

This section presents the investment performance of insurers in 2023. It first looks at their asset allocation and then at the rates of return.

4.1. Bonds accounted for over half of the assets of insurers at end-2023

Bonds accounted for over half of the assets of insurers at end-2023. While asset allocations varied across jurisdictions, life and composite insurers tend to invest the most in fixed-income securities, with a view to matching their long-term liabilities (for life insurance business) and having a stable and regular source of income (Figure 4.1).[20] Insurers generally held more government bonds than corporate bonds, with some exceptions (e.g. France, Chinese Taipei, Switzerland).[21] The higher interest rates in comparison with previous years led some insurers to increase their exposure to bonds to benefit from higher expected future returns, such as in Bulgaria (life insurers), Colombia, Estonia (life insurers), and Peru. In Colombia, life insurers increased their investments in domestic inflation-indexed government bonds in order to protect their portfolios against inflation, as their payments increase with inflation and rises in the minimum wage.

Figure 4.1. Average asset allocation of domestic life, non-life and composite insurers among reporting jurisdictions, at end-2023

As a percentage of total investment

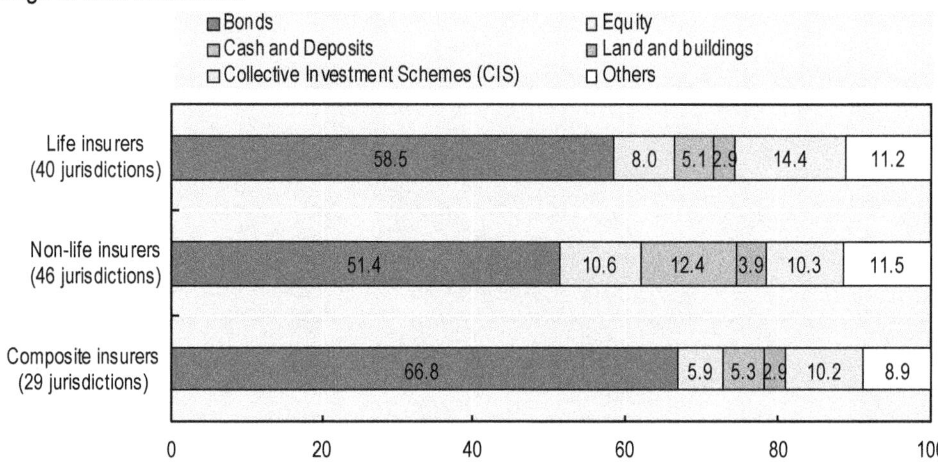

Note: Data exclude assets linked to unit-linked products where risk is fully borne by policyholders. The "Others" category includes investments in loans, private equity funds, hedge funds, structured products and other investments. Negative values in some categories for some jurisdictions were excluded from the calculations of the asset allocation.
Source: OECD Global Insurance Statistics.

StatLink https://stat.link/bdq5ey

While equities accounted for a lower proportion of the investments of insurers, insurers in some jurisdictions still held a significant share of assets in equities. Those with the highest proportion of assets in equities at end-2023 included life insurers in Denmark and Sweden and non-life insurers in Austria, with more than 40% of assets in equities.[22] Non-life insurers held also a relatively high proportion of assets in equities in France (30%), Japan (30%) and the United States (26%).

All insurers also held a portion of their assets in cash and deposits, which are liquid assets. Non-life insurers tend to hold a larger proportion of assets in cash and deposits as they need liquid instruments to meet claims requests. Deposits may have become more attractive due to the higher investment returns they can provide in a context of higher interest rates. Some insurers increased their holdings of cash and deposits when they had, or were expecting to have, more liquidity needs (e.g. life insurers in France, non-life insurers in Slovenia). In France, life insurers slightly increased their cash position to be able to pay for policy surrenders, in order to avoid having to sell undervalued bonds and crystalise losses. In Slovenia, non-life insurers significantly increased their holdings of cash and deposits (by nine percentage points) due to the reform of private health insurance.

Insurers also invested in instruments or vehicles other than bonds, equities and cash and deposits. These alternative investments include for instance land and buildings. For example, the proportion of assets in land and building was relatively high for life insurers in Switzerland (16% of assets) and Norway (10%). Finland reported that real estate investments accounted for 14% of assets of non-life insurers. The relatively high proportion of assets in alternative investments in some jurisdictions may reflect the search for yield by insurers and less liquid investments in a low interest rate environment. Despite interest rates being higher, life insurers continued to invest in private markets to some extent in order to diversify and enhance returns (BIS, 2024[21]).

4.2. Positive trends in financial markets allowed insurers to improve their investment performance

The investment performance of insurers improved in 2023. Insurers achieved a positive real investment rate of return in 23 out 35 jurisdictions (66%) for insurers operating in the life sector only, 23 out 38 (61%) for those operating in the non-life sector, and 16 out of 25 (64%) for those operating in both sectors (Figure 4.2). This contrasts with 2022 when the insurance industry experienced negative real investment rates of return in nearly all jurisdictions (Annex A). In 2023, insurers in Poland and Peru recorded the strongest investment performance in the non-life insurance sector, with real investment rates of return above 10%. Nearly all the jurisdictions with a negative investment rate of return for the industry in 2023 in real terms (e.g. Egypt, Türkiye) had a positive investment rate of return in nominal terms.[23]

Figure 4.2. Average real net investment rates of return by type of domestic insurer in selected jurisdictions in 2023

In per cent

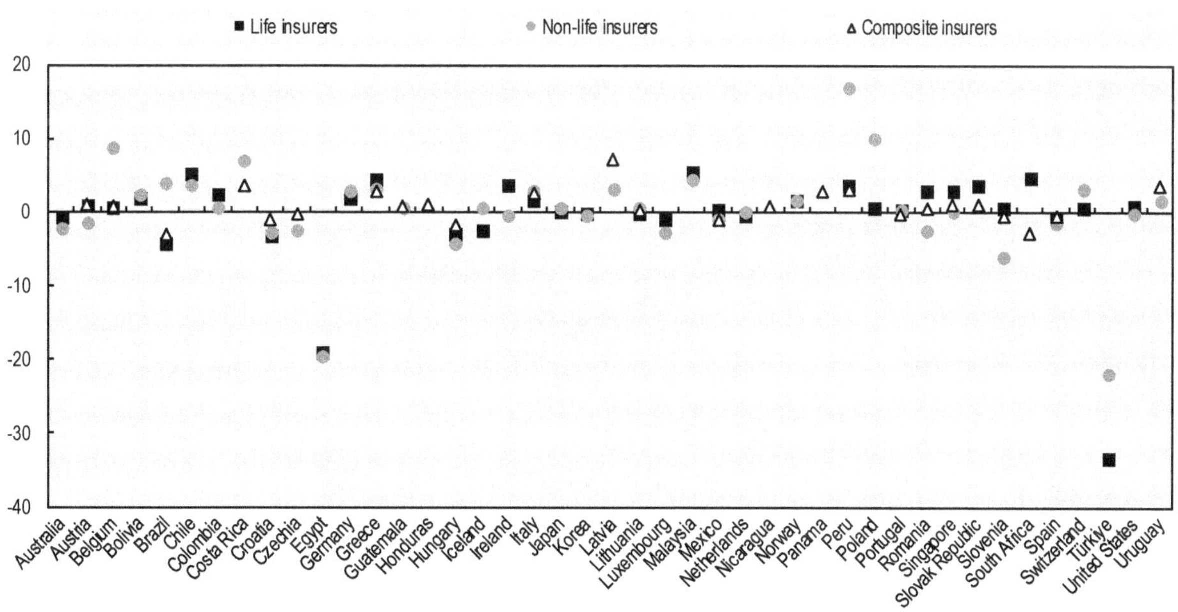

Note: Average annual real net investment rates of return are calculated based on the nominal annual net investment rates of return reported by jurisdictions for 2023 and the variation of the consumer price index over the same period. The investment rates of return of insurers operating in the life insurance section may cover unit-linked products in some cases.
Source: OECD Global Insurance Statistics.

StatLink https://stat.link/z3exks

The positive investment performance of insurers in 2023 was mainly the result of the decline in government bond yields toward the end of 2023 and rising equity valuations. While the yields on long-term government bonds increased and peaked in October 2023 in major advanced economies, they declined in the last quarter of 2023 as investors expected interest rate cuts (BIS, 2024[22]; IMF, 2024[23]). They also fell at the end of 2023 in emerging market economies (BIS, 2024[22]). This decline enabled insurers to record gains in their bond holdings where valued on a mark-to-market basis. Insurers also benefitted from positive developments in equity markets worldwide, with the MSCI World Index for instance rising by 20% in 2023.[24] Some of the jurisdictions where the highest investment rates of return were registered also had a higher proportion of assets allocated to equities, as was the case for non-life insurers in Poland and Peru.

Despite gains on bond and equities, insurers may have faced losses in other asset classes, such as real estate, or due to hedging strategies. For example, in Finland, the downturn in the real estate market in 2023 led to losses in the real estate investments of non-life insurers. In Chinese Taipei, insurers faced higher hedging costs when interest rates were on the rise, lowering investment returns.

The recent implementation of new accounting standards (e.g. IFRS 9 for financial instruments) affected the measurement of investment performance in some jurisdictions. For instance, in Norway, following the adoption of IFRS 9 in 2023, the proportion of assets measured at fair value increased while the proportion held at amortised cost declined.

5 The profitability of insurers broadly improved, with previous negative performance generally reversed

This section presents the overall profitability of insurers in 2023. It first looks at insurer profitability in 2023 based on return on equity (ROE) and then at the evolution of insurer shareholder equity.

5.1. The profitability of insurers broadly improved in 2023

Insurers recorded overall profitability in 2023. The return on equity (ROE), a key measure of corporate profitability, was positive in all jurisdictions for life insurers, 35 out of 37 jurisdictions (95%) for non-life insurers, and 20 out of 21 jurisdictions (95%) for composite insurers (Figure 5.1).[25] This is an improvement compared to 2022 when fewer jurisdictions recorded a positive performance (OECD, 2023[8]).[26] In 2022, the ROE was negative in several jurisdictions due to lower investment performance (OECD, 2023[8]) .

The return on equity was the strongest in Türkiye (driven by a general increase in prices) and several Latin American countries (e.g. Brazil, Guatemala, Peru). Insurers in only two jurisdictions recorded losses in 2023: non-life insurers in Argentina and Slovenia and composite insurers in Argentina.

Figure 5.1. Return on equity by type of insurer in 2023

In per cent

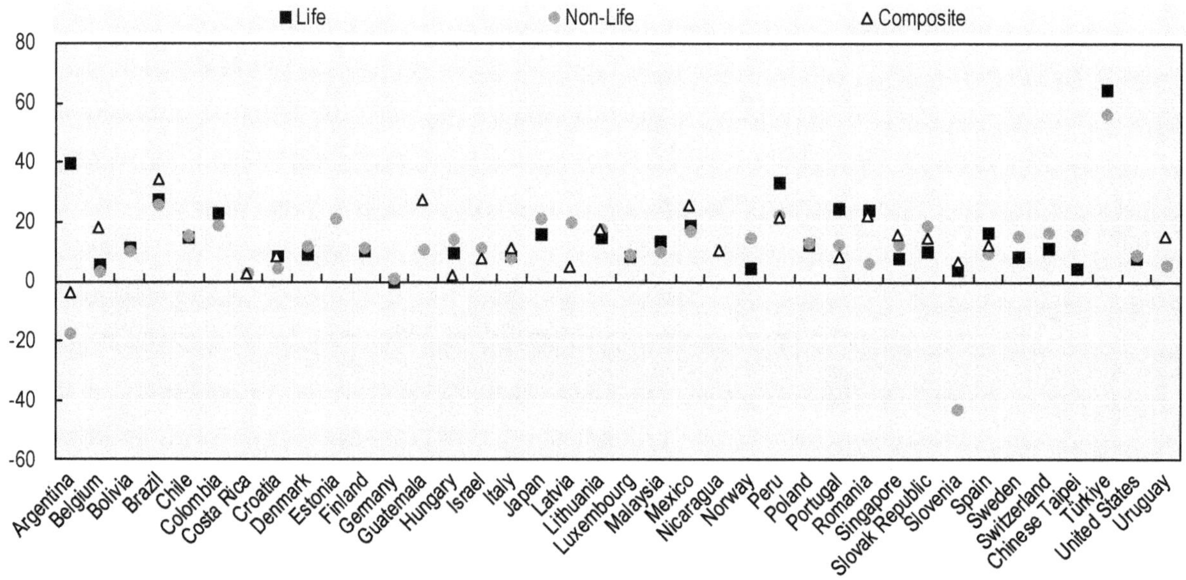

Note: The return on equity (ROE) was calculated by dividing net income in 2023 by the average shareholder equity in 2022 and 2023.
Source: OECD Global Insurance Statistics.

StatLink https://stat.link/w9i1x5

This profitability reflected the positive investment performance that insurers recorded in most jurisdictions in 2023. In a few jurisdictions (e.g. Colombia, Chinese Taipei and Türkiye), for non-life insurers, this positive investment performance offset underwriting losses. Where insurers managed to achieve underwriting gains for the business they wrote, these gains added to their investment gains.

5.2. Insurer shareholder equity generally increased

Insurer shareholder equity increased in most jurisdictions in 2023.[27] Figure 5.2 shows that shareholder equity increased in 27 out of 38 jurisdictions (71%) for life insurers, 37 out of 44 jurisdictions (84%) for non-life insurers and 22 out of 26 jurisdictions (85%) for composite insurers. The highest increase occurred in Argentina and Türkiye (driven by high inflation in these two countries) and Chinese Taipei.

Figure 5.2. Change in shareholder equity by type of insurer in 2023

In per cent

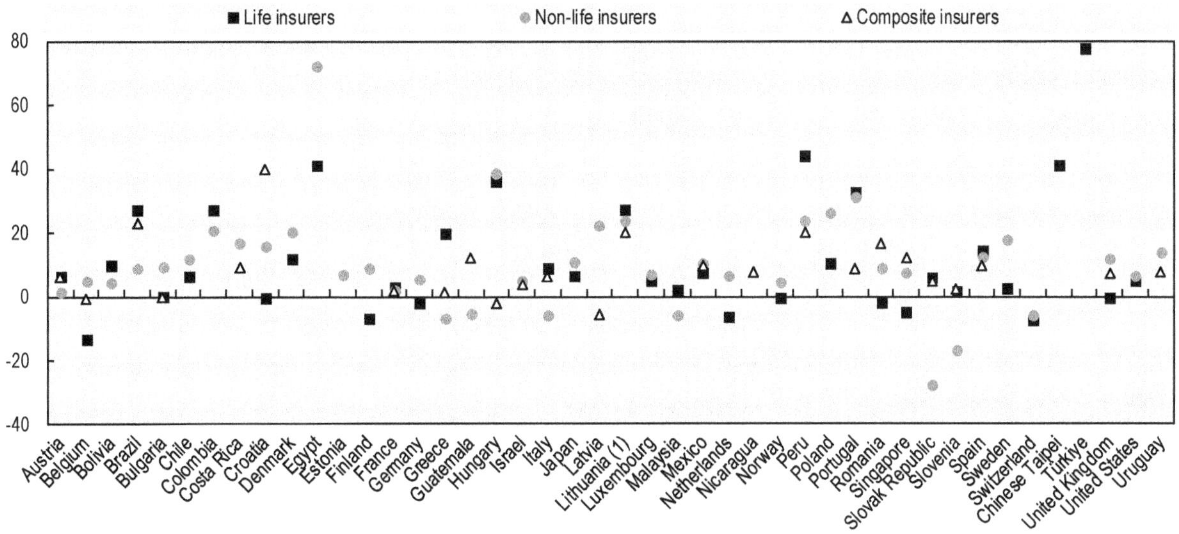

Note: Change in equity position is calculated as the change in shareholder equity divided by the level of shareholder equity of the previous year. For readability purposes, the chart does not show the change in shareholder equity of insurers in Argentina (138.2% for life insurers, 98.1% for non-life insurers and 117.1% for composite insurers), non-life insurers in Chinese Taipei (107.3%) and non-life insurers in Türkiye (119.7%).
1. Data for life insurers exclude the life insurance company that ended its activities in January 2023.
Source: OECD Global Insurance Statistics.

StatLink https://stat.link/y38vh1

Positive insurer profitability in 2023 supported the growth of shareholder equity in 2023. For example, in Chinese Taipei, life insurers experienced an increase in shareholder equity in 2023 due to higher net investment income while, for the non-life sector, shareholder equity rose due to the raising of capital through new share issuance. In Peru, the relatively strong growth of shareholder equity was the result of an increase in net earnings. In Israel, insurer profitability increased earnings available for shareholders, thus contributing to shareholder equity. In Portugal, shareholder equity grew as a result of an improvement of revaluation reserves due to the positive impact of financial markets developments on investments valued at fair value through reserves. In the United States, shareholder equity in the life sector increased due to unrealised capital gains and a decrease in dividends. Stockholder dividends declined by 8% in 2023 (NAIC, 2024[24]).

Share issuance contributed to the evolution of shareholder equity in Chinese Taipei. Shareholder equity increased due to capital-raising in 2023. Life insurers have been issuing subordinated debt since 2023 in order to strengthen their capital position and prepare for new capital requirements (The Asian Business, 2024[25]).

The new accounting standard IFRS 17 for insurance contracts has had an impact on insurer shareholder equity. EIOPA (2024[26]) has found that IFRS 17 generally increased the value of the insurance liabilities (through the use of different discount rates and the introduction of new component of the insurance liabilities), thereby reducing retained earnings which are a component of shareholder equity. While insurers in many European countries started implemented in 2023, some others (e.g. in Latin America) plan to implement it in the coming years (Box 5.1).

Box 5.1. Implementation of new accounting standards in the insurance industry

In 2023, insurers in many countries started implementing IFRS 17, the accounting standard for insurance contracts. It replaces IFRS 4 and sets outs principles for the recognition, measurement, presentation and disclosure of insurance contracts.[1] The objective of IFRS 17 is to enhance transparency and harmonise insurance accounting.

IFRS 17 has multiple implications on the accounting of insurance companies, such as:[2]

- *A transition from a historical to a forward-looking approach to accounting*: Insurers must measure liabilities at market value by calculating the present value of future cash flows. Insurers must reflect the time value of money for all cash flows (e.g. premiums, claims, expenses).
- *Profit recognition at the beginning of insurance contract*: IFRS 17 requires the calculation of the expected profit on the contract and allows insurers to spread it over the lifetime of the contract (contractual service margin).
- *Enhanced disclosure of the sources of profit*: IFRS 17 requires the separation of technical and financial income. It also makes a distinction between recognised and future profit in the financial statements of insurers.
- *Grouping of contracts*: IFRS 17 requires insurers to group contracts together for accounting.

IFRS 17 has a more significant impact on life insurers than on non-life insurers.[3]

The implementation of IFRS 17 is at different stages around the world. While many European countries started implementing IFRS 17 in 2023, jurisdictions in other regions announced they would implement it in the coming years, such as Colombia (2027), Costa Rica (2026), Peru (2028) and Chinese Taipei (2026). Some countries implementing IFRS 17 may apply it only to some insurers. For example, in Poland, IFRS reporting was required only for group statements of publicly traded entities (just one group in Poland). Other insurance entities in Poland either did not need to implement these standards or did so internally, for consolidation purposes of their IFRS-reporting foreign parent entities.

Given the variability that IFRS 17 introduces on the liability side (especially of life insurers), some countries that introduced IFRS 17 decided to implement IFRS 9 at the same time (e.g. Lithuania). IFRS 9 concerns the valuation of financial instruments, specifying how entities should measure financial assets and financial liabilities.[4] Although IFRS 9 has been in effect since 2018, insurers could use a temporary exemption and follow the previous standard that IFRS 9 replaced (IAS 39) until IFRS 17 became effective.[5] The simultaneous implementation of IFRS 9 and 17 can reduce potential inconsistencies and differences in the valuation of assets and liabilities arising from insurance contracts.

Note:

1. IFRS - IFRS 17 Insurance Contracts.
2. This summary is based on the article: The IFRS 17 standard: overview, basic principles and objectives.
3. IFRS 17 real time detailed analysis .
4. IFRS - IFRS 9 Financial Instruments.
5. IFRS 9 for insurers

References

ACPR (2024), *The life insurance market in 2023*, https://acpr.banque-france.fr/en/life-insurance-market-2023. [20]

BIS (2024), *BIS Quarterly Review - September 2024*, https://www.bis.org/publ/qtrpdf/r_qt2409.htm. [21]

BIS (2024), *BIS Quarterly Review, March 2024*, https://www.bis.org/publ/qtrpdf/r_qt2403a.pdf. [22]

Carrier Management (2024), *Climate Losses Batter Insurers While Reinsurers Step Back*, https://www.carriermanagement.com/news/2024/09/05/266196.htm. [17]

Daily Finland (2022), "Reimbursements for private medical costs to change from Jan", *Daily Finland*. [12]

Dirección General de Seguros y Fondos de Pensiones (2024), *Seguros y Fondos de Pensiones - Informe 2023*, https://dgsfp.mineco.gob.es/es/Publicaciones/DocumentosPublicaciones/V6%20Memoria%20informe%20del%20sector%202023.pdf. [18]

EIOPA (2024), *Financial Stability Report June 2024*, https://www.eiopa.europa.eu/publications/financial-stability-report-june-2024_en. [15]

EIOPA (2024), *Report on the implementation of IFRS 17 - Insurance contracts*, https://www.eiopa.europa.eu/publications/report-implementation-ifrs-17-insurance-contracts_en. [26]

Fitch (2023), *Reinsurers' Underwriting Margins to Expand by 4pp in 2023*, https://www.fitchratings.com/research/insurance/reinsurers-underwriting-margins-to-expand-by-4pp-in-2023-10-01-2023. [16]

Fong, J. and J. Li (2022), "Mandatory annuitization and money's worth: evidence from Singapore", *Journal of Pension Economics and Finance*, Vol. 21/3, pp. 405-424, https://doi.org/10.1017/S147474722100010X. [5]

IMF (2024), *Costa Rica: Technical Assistance Report-Universal Basic Pension: Objectives and Constraints*, https://doi.org/10.5089/9798400276705.019. [6]

IMF (2024), *Global Financial Stability Report: The Last Mile: Financial Vulnerabilities and Risks*. [23]

IMF (2024), *World Economic Outlook: Policy Pivot, Rising Threats*, https://www.imf.org/en/Publications/WEO/Issues/2024/10/22/world-economic-outlook-october-2024. [9]

Insurance Journal (2024), "Turkey Earthquake Tops 2023 Insurance Industry Losses Outside US: CRESTA", *Insurance Journal*. [14]

Kwon, W. and L. Wolfrom (2017), *Analytical tools for the insurance market and macro-prudential surveillance*, https://doi.org/10.1787/fmt-2016-5jln6hnvwdzn. [1]

MAPFRE (2022), *Insurance accounts for more than 7% of the global economy*, https://www.mapfre.com/en/insights/insurance/insurance-accounts-for-more-than-seven-percent-the-global-economy/. [2]

NAIC (2024), *U.S. Life and A&H Insurance Industry - 2023 Annual Results*, https://content.naic.org/sites/default/files/topics-industry-snapshot-analysis-reports-2023-annual-report-life.pdf. [24]

NAIC (2024), *U.S. Property & Casualty and Title Insurance Industries – 2023 Full Year Results*, https://content.naic.org/sites/default/files/inline-files/2023%20Annual%20Property%20%26%20Casualty%20Insurance%20Industries%20Analysis%20Report.pdf. [11]

OECD (2024), *Pension Markets in Focus 2024*, OECD Publishing, Paris, https://doi.org/10.1787/b11473d3-en. [19]

OECD (2023), *Global Insurance Market Trends 2023*, OECD Publishing, Paris, https://doi.org/10.1787/e141d5ff-en. [8]

OECD (2023), *Health at a Glance 2023: OECD Indicators*, OECD Publishing, Paris, https://doi.org/10.1787/7a7afb35-en. [4]

OECD (2022), *Private health insurance spending*, https://www.oecd.org/en/publications/private-health-insurance-spending_4985356e-en.html. [3]

OECD (2016), *Life Annuity Products and Their Guarantees*, OECD Publishing, Paris, https://doi.org/10.1787/9789264265318-en. [7]

Swiss Re (2024), *New record of 142 natural catastrophes accumulates to USD 108 billion insured losses in 2023, finds Swiss Re Institute*, https://www.swissre.com/press-release/New-record-of-142-natural-catastrophes-accumulates-to-USD-108-billion-insured-losses-in-2023-finds-Swiss-Re-Institute/a2512914-6d3a-492e-a190-aac37feca15b#:%7E:text=2023%20was%20also%20marked%20by,were%20SCS%2C%20a%20. [10]

The Asian Business (2024), *Taiwan insurers to raise fresh equity amidst new capital requirement*, https://asianbusinessreview.com/insurance/news/taiwan-insurers-raise-fresh-equity-amidst-new-capital-requirement. [25]

Yle (2024), *Insurance payouts surge due to harsh winter, growing private health coverage*, https://yle.fi/a/74-20109670. [13]

Annex A. Statistical tables

Table A A.1. Asset allocation of domestic life insurers in main instruments or vehicles, at end-2023

As a percentage of total investment

	Bonds	Equity	Cash and Deposits	Land and buildings	Collective Investment Schemes (CIS)	Others
Argentina	59.9	2.2	0.4	5.8	29.3	2.4
Australia	67.8	18.1	4.8	7.2	0.0	2.1
Austria	39.6	1.8	3.4	0.3	50.7	4.2
Belgium	47.6	9.5	1.9	2.4	21.9	16.8
Bolivia	62.3	2.2	4.6	20.4	0.0	10.5
Brazil	51.4	0.2	1.1	0.1	40.3	6.9
Bulgaria	9.3	13.8	5.4	0.0	71.5	0.0
Chile	51.0	0.7	2.5	8.3	11.5	25.9
Colombia	75.0	4.2	2.4	0.0	3.0	15.4
Croatia	63.1	1.5	25.0	3.4	7.0	0.0
Denmark	29.9	46.7	2.8	0.4	5.3	15.1
Finland	55.1	6.9	13.5	5.5	16.0	3.0
France	59.9	8.9	2.5	2.4	17.9	8.3
Germany	35.2	11.9	1.2	1.6	39.1	11.0
Greece	62.8	18.1	4.5	0.0	13.3	1.3
Hungary	86.7	1.6	1.6	0.4	6.9	2.7
Italy	80.2	2.5	1.3	0.2	11.1	4.7
Japan	65.0	9.2	2.4	1.5	0.0	22.0
Korea	49.5	5.9	2.4	1.5	0.0	40.7
Lithuania	70.5	0.0	13.6	0.0	13.7	2.2
Luxembourg	31.1	3.1	3.4	0.0	8.8	53.5
Malaysia	67.7	11.2	4.4	1.7	0.0	15.0
Mexico	95.9	0.0	0.1	0.1	0.1	3.8
Netherlands	37.1	8.4	4.8	1.4	12.3	36.0
Norway	46.4	9.7	0.4	9.6	19.1	14.8
Peru	77.1	4.2	4.4	7.9	4.5	1.9
Poland	73.4	5.0	3.1	0.4	11.1	7.1
Portugal	84.1	4.0	2.2	2.0	4.3	3.4
Romania	92.0	1.9	4.8	0.2	0.8	0.2
Singapore	56.4	11.5	2.9	1.5	24.4	3.4
Slovak Republic	56.0	15.6	14.4	1.5	12.5	0.0
Slovenia	91.5	0.8	4.3	0.4	3.1	0.0
South Africa	15.7	13.2	5.5	0.1	54.7	10.7
Spain	70.8	4.5	3.9	1.9	6.0	12.9
Sweden	25.6	40.1	3.2	1.3	20.5	9.3
Switzerland	50.8	3.6	2.9	15.7	4.9	22.2
Chinese Taipei	66.3	7.6	1.7	5.5	4.2	14.8
Türkiye	49.4	2.4	34.3	0.6	12.6	0.7

	Bonds	Equity	Cash and Deposits	Land and buildings	Collective Investment Schemes (CIS)	Others
United Kingdom	61.2	2.8	1.8	0.9	12.5	20.8
United States	68.4	4.0	3.3	0.4	0.0	23.9

Note: Data exclude assets linked to unit-linked products where risk is fully borne by policyholders. The "Others" category includes investments in loans, private equity funds, hedge funds, structured products and other investments. Negative values in some categories for some jurisdictions were excluded from the calculations of the asset allocation.
Source: OECD Global Insurance Statistics.

StatLink https://stat.link/frtzl8

Table A A.2. Asset allocation of domestic non-life insurers in main instruments or vehicles, at end-2023

As a percentage of total investment

	Bonds	Equity	Cash and Deposits	Land and buildings	Collective Investment Schemes (CIS)	Others
Argentina	54.2	3.7	1.8	5.3	31.8	3.1
Australia	66.8	2.6	8.5	0.3	17.8	4.1
Austria (1)	6.8	65.0	10.7	4.2	11.3	2.1
Belgium	56.1	6.5	9.5	2.0	20.7	5.2
Bolivia	70.0	2.9	4.5	19.2	0.0	3.4
Brazil	58.7	0.0	1.7	0.3	37.8	1.5
Bulgaria	50.8	4.8	17.8	6.4	16.8	3.4
Chile	67.1	0.9	19.0	3.2	5.2	4.5
Colombia	61.2	9.0	6.7	0.0	4.4	18.7
Costa Rica	62.5	0.5	15.2	0.0	0.0	21.8
Croatia	10.5	22.9	14.3	35.4	1.3	15.6
Czechia	48.0	12.3	27.2	2.3	2.0	8.2
Denmark	41.4	14.6	25.4	1.1	10.1	7.3
Estonia	80.4	0.1	17.1	0.0	1.5	0.9
Finland	23.0	15.4	5.4	5.0	35.9	15.3
France	39.9	30.4	5.3	2.2	15.8	6.3
Germany	38.5	16.9	1.9	1.4	34.7	6.5
Greece	58.3	8.0	8.2	6.8	17.4	1.2
Guatemala	44.3	0.4	45.8	4.9	0.0	4.5
Hungary	80.9	0.0	10.9	1.4	0.9	5.9
Israel	38.7	2.7	9.7	2.0	27.6	19.2
Italy	78.1	5.8	4.2	2.6	8.8	0.4
Japan	18.0	30.4	6.3	2.7	0.0	42.7
Korea	37.2	4.8	2.9	1.6	0.0	53.4
Latvia	74.2	4.2	8.4	3.3	6.7	3.2
Lithuania	80.6	1.2	5.8	2.0	5.4	5.1
Luxembourg	40.6	1.4	4.0	1.2	1.7	51.0
Malaysia	30.2	1.3	21.4	1.0	0.0	46.1
Mexico	79.7	1.7	4.3	4.4	1.0	8.8
Netherlands	42.8	16.8	6.9	0.4	23.9	9.2
Norway	55.6	8.6	5.1	6.1	21.9	2.7

	Bonds	Equity	Cash and Deposits	Land and buildings	Collective Investment Schemes (CIS)	Others
Peru	30.4	25.1	13.9	3.5	5.9	21.2
Poland	57.6	26.1	2.1	0.3	9.6	4.2
Portugal	71.2	7.4	11.2	3.2	4.1	2.8
Romania	71.0	3.1	24.9	0.6	0.1	0.3
Singapore	44.1	1.6	40.4	1.3	3.7	9.0
Slovenia	75.4	4.4	13.7	4.9	1.6	0.0
South Africa	29.7	6.6	20.1	0.5	12.5	30.6
Spain	51.9	15.6	10.6	7.3	10.3	4.3
Sweden	29.3	34.1	3.9	3.9	23.1	5.7
Switzerland	32.7	4.3	5.3	4.9	7.3	45.6
Chinese Taipei	45.4	15.5	9.9	14.3	2.5	12.4
Türkiye	23.6	12.4	50.8	1.2	11.9	0.0
United Kingdom	63.2	10.2	7.3	1.9	16.5	1.0
United States	56.4	25.9	9.5	0.7	0.0	7.5
Uruguay	88.0	0.2	11.2	0.0	0.0	0.5

Note: The "Others" category includes investments in loans, private equity funds, hedge funds, structured products and other investments. Negative values in some categories for some jurisdictions were excluded from the calculations of the asset allocation. (1) The high proportion of assets in equity is due to participations in other undertakings, which account for most of equity investments.
Source: OECD Global Insurance Statistics.

StatLink https://stat.link/aljnxf

Table A A.3. Asset allocation of domestic composite insurers in main instruments or vehicles, at end-2023

As a percentage of total investment

	Bonds	Equity	Cash and Deposits	Land and buildings	Collective Investment Schemes (CIS)	Others
Argentina	48.1	7.5	3.2	7.6	29.8	3.8
Austria	45.4	14.5	1.8	11.7	20.3	6.4
Belgium	61.9	7.3	2.2	3.3	7.6	17.7
Brazil	54.0	1.9	1.0	0.2	29.8	13.0
Bulgaria	87.1	0.1	3.2	3.6	5.3	0.7
Costa Rica	73.7	5.7	5.9	0.0	1.1	13.5
Croatia	68.1	10.1	3.6	9.6	4.6	3.9
Czechia	71.8	9.4	6.0	0.3	5.6	6.9
Estonia	68.1	0.6	7.3	0.0	12.3	11.8
France	56.1	8.6	2.8	1.4	23.3	7.8
Greece	79.4	2.4	4.5	2.3	10.1	1.3
Guatemala	54.8	1.4	27.6	4.1	0.0	12.0
Hungary	76.3	1.4	8.9	4.0	2.0	7.4
Israel	53.1	3.8	6.6	4.9	3.6	28.0
Italy	66.8	10.2	1.6	0.7	15.7	5.0
Latvia	44.5	8.0	15.0	0.0	32.0	0.5
Lithuania	70.9	6.8	2.5	0.0	8.7	11.0
Mexico	62.3	1.3	0.9	1.5	27.5	6.6

	Bonds	Equity	Cash and Deposits	Land and buildings	Collective Investment Schemes (CIS)	Others
Nicaragua	81.8	0.1	2.3	3.0	0.4	12.3
Peru	75.2	2.9	3.5	8.2	4.1	6.1
Portugal	60.7	23.8	3.6	1.5	6.3	4.1
Romania	81.6	6.0	8.7	0.4	1.9	1.3
Singapore	67.3	7.6	3.3	1.9	17.5	2.4
Slovak Republic	79.1	5.1	7.2	4.3	1.5	2.8
Slovenia	68.9	14.0	1.6	5.5	8.1	2.0
South Africa	34.9	0.5	11.3	0.0	0.5	52.8
Spain	79.4	6.2	3.5	4.1	3.2	3.6
United Kingdom	75.9	3.7	3.2	0.7	11.1	5.3
Uruguay	91.0	0.1	0.4	0.2	1.4	7.0

Note: Data exclude assets linked to unit-linked products where risk is fully borne by policyholders. The "Others" category includes investments in loans, private equity funds, hedge funds, structured products and other investments. Negative values in some categories for some jurisdictions were excluded from the calculations of the asset allocation.
Source: OECD Global Insurance Statistics.

StatLink https://stat.link/do8g5s

Table A A.4. Average nominal and real net investment rates of return by type of domestic insurer in 2022 and 2023

In per cent

	Nominal						Real					
	Life		Non-Life		Composite		Life		Non-Life		Composite	
	2022	2023	2022	2023	2022	2023	2022	2023	2022	2023	2022	2023
Argentina	48.7	95.1	53.9	86.6	49.7	89.3	..	..	..	..	..	..
Australia	-7.3	5.5	-3.1	3.7	..	..	-12.6	-0.5	-8.7	-2.2	..	..
Austria	-22.4	6.7	-0.5	4.1	-13.2	6.8	-29.6	1.0	-9.6	-1.4	-21.2	1.2
Belgium	-2.2	1.9	5.6	10.3	2.5	2.3	-11.4	0.5	-4.3	8.8	-7.2	0.9
Bolivia	3.9	4.0	4.2	4.6	..	..	0.8	1.9	1.0	2.4	..	..
Brazil	0.4	0.3	9.6	8.8	1.2	1.3	-5.1	-4.2	3.6	4.0	-4.3	-3.2
Chile	..	..	..	..	..	..	4.5	5.2	2.8	3.8	..	..
Colombia	10.2	12.0	5.5	10.0	..	..	-2.5	2.5	-6.7	0.7	..	..
Costa Rica	..	..	2.6	5.3	3.5	1.7	..	..	-4.9	7.1	-4.1	3.5
Croatia	2.3	1.3	2.1	1.8	1.8	3.4	-9.5	-3.1	-9.7	-2.6	-10.0	-1.1
Czechia	c	c	3.1	4.2	2.1	6.7	c	c	-10.9	-2.5	-11.8	-0.1
Denmark	-14.3	..	..	..	..	..	-21.2	..	..	..	..	..
Egypt	8.4	10.0	10.0	9.3	..	..	-4.2	-19.0	-2.7	-19.5	..	..
El Salvador	3.8	..	6.2	..	3.6	..	-3.3	..	-1.0	..	-3.4	..
Estonia	c	..	-6.0	..	..	..	c	..	-20.1	..	..	..
Germany	-22.2	5.8	-13.5	6.9	..	..	-28.0	2.1	-20.0	3.1	..	..
Greece	..	8.2	..	6.8	..	6.3	..	4.5	..	3.2	..	2.7
Guatemala	..	..	4.8	4.8	5.2	5.0	..	..	-4.0	0.7	-3.7	0.9
Honduras	..	..	..	..	3.1	6.3	..	..	..	..	-6.1	1.0
Hungary	3.6	2.5	1.5	1.1	3.9	3.8	-16.8	-2.9	-18.5	-4.2	-16.6	-1.7
Iceland	0.5	5.1	3.2	8.4	..	..	-8.3	-2.4	-5.8	0.6	..	..
Ireland	-14.0	8.4	-5.0	4.2	..	..	-20.5	3.7	-12.2	-0.4	..	..

Italy	0.3	2.4	-2.7	3.6	2.0	3.2	-10.2	1.8	-12.8	3.0	-8.6	2.6
Japan	2.2	2.8	2.9	3.5	..	..	-1.0	0.1	-0.4	0.8	..	..
Korea	3.0	3.1	3.1	2.7	..	..	-1.9	-0.1	-1.8	-0.5	..	..
Latvia	..	..	-2.8	3.8	-15.9	7.8	..	..	-19.6	3.2	-30.4	7.1
Lithuania	4.4	1.1	-1.1	1.9	2.0	1.6	-14.2	-0.1	-18.7	0.7	-16.2	0.4
Luxembourg	1.1	2.6	0.8	0.7	..	..	-4.1	-0.9	-4.4	-2.8	..	..
Malaysia	0.7	7.3	3.5	6.1	..	..	-3.0	5.6	-0.3	4.5	..	..
Mexico	5.6	5.1	4.1	3.7	3.9	3.5	-2.0	0.4	-3.4	-0.9	-3.7	-1.1
Netherlands	-3.2	0.8	-1.8	1.3	..	..	-11.6	-0.4	-10.4	0.1	..	..
Nicaragua	..	..	..	..	6.6	6.4	..	..	..	..	-4.5	0.7
Norway	-3.0	6.5	3.3	6.5	..	..	-8.4	1.6	-2.5	1.6	..	..
Panama	..	..	..	..	3.3	4.8	..	..	..	..	1.2	2.8
Peru	7.4	7.2	11.5	20.9	4.3	6.5	-1.1	3.7	2.7	16.9	-3.9	3.0
Poland	-2.5	7.0	-1.9	16.9	..	..	-16.5	0.7	-16.0	10.1	..	..
Portugal	-2.3	1.9	-5.3	1.8	0.3	1.1	-10.9	0.5	-13.6	0.4	-8.5	-0.3
Romania	-4.2	9.8	-0.7	4.0	-1.9	7.2	-17.7	2.9	-14.7	-2.5	-15.7	0.6
Singapore	-12.4	6.8	-1.8	3.9	-13.8	4.9	-17.7	3.0	-7.8	0.2	-19.1	1.1
Slovak Republic	-15.2	9.8	..	..	-18.6	7.0	-26.5	3.7	..	..	-29.4	1.0
Slovenia	-2.1	4.9	-1.2	-2.1	-0.1	3.7	-11.2	0.7	-10.4	-6.0	-9.4	-0.4
South Africa	3.2	10.2	..	..	1.7	2.2	-4.0	4.8	..	..	-5.4	-2.8
Spain	2.0	2.5	1.0	1.6	1.9	2.7	-3.5	-0.6	-4.4	-1.5	-3.6	-0.4
Switzerland	1.1	2.3	3.3	4.9	..	..	-1.7	0.6	0.4	3.2	..	..
Chinese Taipei	3.3	3.0	2.8	3.0	..	..	..	..	..	..	..	..
Türkiye	7.8	10.0	22.6	29.0	..	..	-34.4	-33.2	-25.4	-21.7	..	..
United States	4.1	4.3	3.1	3.2	..	..	-2.2	0.9	-3.2	-0.1	..	..
Uruguay	..	..	0.8	6.9	8.4	9.0	..	..	-6.9	1.7	0.1	3.7

Source: OECD Global Insurance Statistics.

StatLink https://stat.link/il1rgz

Annex B. Methodological notes

This report is mainly based on the data and responses from the jurisdictions participating in the annual Global Insurance Statistics (GIS) exercise. Data collected under the GIS exercise are accessible at: OECD Data Explorer.

Data in this report may diverge from the short preview of insurance trends published in July 2024. This preview was based on early estimates for domestic undertakings only, sometimes coming from other sources than in this report.

Some divergences may also exist between national reporting standards and the data compilation method in the GIS exercise. For this reason, jurisdictions are regularly requested to provide relevant methodological information for a thorough understanding of their submissions to the GIS exercise. The methodological notes below provide the main explanations in this respect.

- Conventional signs: "c" means confidential; ".." means missing value (not available or not applicable).
- GDP values come from the “Annual GDP and components - expenditure approach” database for OECD countries; and from the IMF World Economic Outlook released in April 2024 for non-OECD jurisdictions.
- Economic data on the Consumer Price Index (CPI) come from the OECD Consumer Price Indices and the IMF International Financial Statistics (IFS) databases.
- Data in this report generally refer to direct business and include domestically incorporated undertakings (i.e. incorporated under national law) and, where data are available, branches and agencies of foreign undertakings operating in the country. Tables and figures on the asset allocation of insurers and their investment rates of return refer to domestic direct insurers only. Some jurisdictions may be unable to exclude foreign branches of domestic undertakings; therefore, their data may include these foreign branches.
- Composite undertakings operate in a number of jurisdictions. In some jurisdictions, such as Costa Rica, most insurance companies are composite companies dealing with both life and non-life businesses.
- Data on stock variables refer to the end of the year while data on flow variables cover the whole year in the report. The reference period is the calendar year, except for Australia, Argentina, Egypt and Paraguay (12-month period ending in June of the year considered), and Japan (12-month period ending in March of the following year).
- Data for Malaysia cover conventional and takaful insurance products, unless specified otherwise.
- Data on composite insurers from Bulgaria, Italy and Portugal include life insurers also operating in the accident and health line of business.
- Data for Korea's non-life insurance sector include private pension products offered by non-life insurers. Private pension products are considered as life insurance products under OECD definitions.
- Data for the Netherlands cover both basic and additional health insurance.

Notes

[1] Compulsory Automobile Liability Insurance

[2] Car Insurance Requirements by State | Progressive

[3] When it plays a secondary role, private health insurance may cover some remaining costs after basic coverage from the public healthcare system (complementary insurance), provide additional services (supplementary insurance) or give faster access or larger choice of providers (duplicate insurance).

[4] In Chile, people opting out of the public health care coverage have to take up private health insurance coverage for a minimum of services. In France, private-sector employers have had to offer a complementary private health insurance to their employees since 2016. In Germany, public health care coverage is the norm. However, people opting out of the public health care coverage have to take up private health insurance coverage, which is substitutive in terms of services.

[5] Employment-based insurance is the most common type of private health coverage in the United States (with 53.7% of the population covered) followed by Medicaid (18.9%) and Medicare (18.9%). See Health Insurance Coverage in the United States: 2023

[6] Property Insurance Market Size, Share, Trends & Growth 2031

[7] Is Home Insurance Mandatory? | Compare the Market and Property Insurance: Definition and How Coverage Works.

[8] See Insurance Authority - Annual Long Term Business Statistics (Hong Kong (China), Statistics | The Life Insurance Association of Japan (Japan) and Statistics- Insurance Bureau, Financial Supervisory Commission (Chinese Taipei).

[9] Life insurance - Asia | Statista Market Forecast

[10] Malaysian authorities attributed the rise in car sales to promotional campaigns and the launch of new car models (e.g. electric cars).

[11] GI in Japan: Trends, Data and Predictions from GlobalData -

[12] Small insurers were offering policies at a lower price to maintain their market share. This has led to a decline in the average price of motor vehicle insurance policies: Motor insurance segment in S. Korea to exceed $19b by 2028: GlobalData | Insurance Asia

[13] In April 2023, one insurance company offering supplementary health insurance policies announced a 30% increase in premium rates. After that announcement, the Slovenian government intervened and capped the maximum premium rate for all Slovenian insurance companies selling these policies, allowing only a 3.4% increase.

[14] See Insurance Inflation: How & Why Rates Are Affected. For example, the cost of motor vehicle maintenance and repairs in the United States was up by 13% in June 2023 compared to the year before: Cost of Insurance: Why is it rising and what you can do.

[15] See Presentación de PowerPoint (for Mexico). Romania has an 8% cap on sales commissions.

[16] In Finland, the combined ratio improved because of a change in the calculation methodology. The combined ratio would have deteriorated without this change.

[17] 'Milestone' year as annuity sales hit record high - Pensions Age Magazine (for the United Kingdom) and sigma 2/2024: Life insurance in the higher interest rate era | Swiss Re (for the United States).

[18] The trends in payouts depend on the conditions triggering payouts and the type of payments, which can vary across products. Payouts can happen upon the death of policyholders and the maturity or the surrender of the policy. For example, the death of a policyholder of a whole life insurance triggers payments to beneficiaries. Policyholders can receive payments from their endowment policies after a specific term (maturity of the contract). Policyholders can surrender any life insurance policy but may face penalties. Payouts may take different forms such as a single payout (i.e. lump sum) or regular payments. The value may be fixed or indexed (e.g. inflation).

[19] Insurance Statistics 2021 - 2023

[20] See Annex A for the asset allocation of life, non-life and composite insurers by jurisdiction.

[21] In Chinese Taipei, insurers also invest largely in corporate and financial sector bonds, available in high volumes and with a long-term horizon.

[22] In Austria, most of the equity investments of non-life insurers are participations in other undertakings. These participations represent strategic holdings rather than speculative or high-risk assets.

[23] The only exception is Slovenia where non-life insurers recorded a negative investment performance in nominal terms in 2023. This negative performance was due to the extraordinary sale of certain instruments that was necessary to increase capital and meet liquidity needs in the context of the reform of private health insurance in 2023.

[24] MSCI all-country world stocks. See Markets in 2023: Soaring stocks and roaring bonds defy the doubters | Reuters

[25] The return on equity (ROE) is a measure of profitability and income-generating capacity of insurers. It shows how much income insurance companies have generated with the capital that shareholders invested. It is calculated in this report as the net income of the year under review divided by the average of the

shareholder equity of that year and the previous one, as reported on the balance sheet of insurers aggregated at the national level.

[26] In 2022, the ROE was positive in 31 out of 37 reporting jurisdictions for life insurers, in 37 out of 43 for non-life insurers and in 20 out of 23 for composite insurers.

[27] Changes in shareholder equity can arise for various reasons. Shareholder equity declines when insurers distribute cash dividends (as these dividends reduce retained capital earnings) and when insurers purchase their own outstanding shares (buybacks). By contrast, shareholder equity increases when insurers raise capital by issuing new shares. Changes in shareholder equity can also reflect unrecognised gains or losses that do not appear in the income statement but nonetheless may be important to understand the undertaking's financial position. For instance, unrealised gains and losses on investments held to maturity within an investment portfolio do not appear in the income statement, yet they are reflected in changes to shareholder equity. An increase in shareholder equity can reflect a positive net income for insurers.

www.ingramcontent.com/pod-product-compliance
Lightning Source LLC
Chambersburg PA
CBHW061225240926
51846CB00006B/1365
* 9 7 8 9 2 6 4 9 2 2 9 9 0 *